CONSCIENCE IN
NEWMAN'S THOUGHT

CONSCIENCE IN NEWMAN'S THOUGHT

S. A. Grave

CLARENDON PRESS · OXFORD
1989

Oxford University Press, Walton Street, Oxford OX2 6DP

Oxford New York Toronto
Delhi Bombay Calcutta Madras Karachi
Petaling Jaya Singapore Hong Kong Tokyo
Nairobi Dar es Salaam Cape Town
Melbourne Auckland

and associated companies in
Berlin Ibadan

Oxford is a trade mark of Oxford University Press

Published in the United States
by Oxford University Press, New York

© S. A. Grave 1989

British Library Cataloguing in Publication Data

Grave, S. A. (Selwyn Alfred), 1916–
Conscience in Newman's thought
1. Conscience. Christian viewpoints
I. Title
241'.1
ISBN 0–19–824856–3

Library of Congress Cataloging in Publication Data
Data available

Set by Litho Link Limited, Welshpool
Printed and bound in
Great Britain by Biddles Ltd.
Guildford and King's Lynn

ACKNOWLEDGEMENTS

I HAVE to thank Mary Fearnley-Sander, Patience Hook, and Peter Forrest for commenting upon a draft of this essay; also the Superior of the Birmingham Oratory, and its Librarian for giving me access to the Newman archives.

S.A.G.

CONTENTS

INTRODUCTION

I

WHATEVER value there might be in the remark that the Second
Vatican Council was 'Newman, come true', there is no doubt
that the influence of Newman after the Council was far less
than many expected. And a certain influence that he did have
would not have been foreseen, either. While attention to him
as a Catholic apologist, so far from increasing, fell away, his
exaltation of conscience took on in some circles a significance
he would not have understood it to possess. Before beginning
our enquiry into Newman's conception of conscience and its
implications, we shall look for a moment at the Newman who
had lost importance. One of our concerns is the relation
between Newman's thought about conscience and about the
Church, and his most original thinking about the Church
should not be left quite without mention.

With his *Essay on the Development of Christian Doctrine*
(1845) Newman left the Church of England for the Roman
Catholic Church. The *Essay* did pre-eminently two things:
one was to turn the great Anglican counter to Roman
Catholicism against Anglicanism itself; the other to show how
Catholic doctrine had to be seen, and could be seen, if the
principle governing the counter was not to be fatal to Roman
Catholicism and to historical Christianity altogether.

This Anglican counter to Roman Catholicism was 'the
appeal to Antiquity'. Governing the appeal was the 'quod
semper, quod ubique, quod ab omnibus' of the 'Vincentian
principle': the doctrine of Antiquity was that which had been
held 'always, everywhere, and by all', this concurrence
testifying to its Apostolic origin. The force of the appeal is
nowhere conveyed better than by some Anglican words of
Newman's which he reproduced in the Advertisement to the
Essay from one of the Tracts for the Times: how was it
possible to withstand Rome but for 'the anathema of St. Paul

even against Angels and Apostles who should bring in a new doctrine'? Anglican controversialists saw the Roman Catholic doctrines from which they dissented as new.

These doctrines could plausibly be seen as new, the *Essay* concedes; but so also, and sometimes more plausibly, could doctrines of orthodox Protestantism. In 'one sense' the Vincentian principle is 'irresistible against Rome . . . but in the same sense it is irresistible against England. It strikes at Rome through England. It admits of being interpreted in one of two ways . . . if it be relaxed to admit the doctrines retained by the English Church, it no longer excludes certain doctrines of Rome which that Church denies.'[1] Understand the principle in a different sense, as allowing development (as living things develop without losing their identity), and it cannot be invoked against Rome. See the doctrines common to Roman Catholicism and Protestantism, and those that are distinctively Roman Catholic, as the result of a growing comprehension of what was originally given, coming about with time, and as circumstances bring different aspects of it into view, and by its definition in controversy; see these doctrines in that way, and it can be seen that 'the Christianity of the second, fourth, seventh, twelfth, sixteenth, and intermediate centuries is in substance the very religion which Christ and His Apostles taught in the first' (p. 5).

It would be going beyond our purpose to say anything of Newman's handling of the problems in the idea of the development of doctrine; all that was called for was some indication (necessarily abstract) as to what had been regarded as especially important in his thought about the Christian religion, and about the Catholic and Anglican Churches in particular. This having been given, why the expected interest in Newman failed to materialize can be indicated. One reason lay in the theological primitivism which came into being in the Catholic Church after the Second Vatican Council. Conflicting with Newman's thought in fundamental principle was the emergence in that Church of one of the forces which operated in the Reformation, the desire and demand to go back to the

---

[1] *Essay on the Development of Doctrine* (1878 edn.), introd., pp. 11–12. Except as otherwise indicated, quotations from Newman are taken from the edn. of his works published by Longmans, Green and Co. (London, 1868–81).

beginning—'Ad fontes'. In the ecumenist atmosphere which developed after the Council we have the other notable reason. In this atmosphere it was difficult to feel that the question whether the Roman Catholic Church was uniquely the Church established by Christ could have the vast importance it had for Newman; there was little to occasion the question at all. The book with which Newman's name is most closely associated, the *Apologia pro Vita Sua,* with its account of his conversion, would become a book for those interested in understanding the Victorian mind.

Though, for one or other or both of the reason indicated, Newman's most historically significant views could seem theologically anachronistic, his teaching on conscience could seem to be of great moment for our day. Interest in Newman's ideas on conscience is, of course, by no means only recent. Two propositions in Henri Bremond's celebrated work, *Newman: Essai de biographie psychologique,* published in 1906, are that the whole of Newman's philosophy 'is aimed at establishing a fundamental identity between the voice of conscience and the voice of God', and 'the whole of his theology at showing in the God of revelation the God of conscience'.[2]

Newman made great claims for conscience. Obviously, not on behalf of whatever anyone might call 'conscience'. Obviously —to apply in this connection a phrase of Newman's—on behalf of conscience in 'the ordinary sense of the word'. The conscience which he argues could not come into collision with the Church's infallible teaching is again, surely, conscience in this sense of the word. At several points in his argument the assumption is made that the deliverances of conscience are of a certain character; at such significant points that if the assumption is rejected there is no argument left. How is the assumption to be tested? It would have to be tested against the character possessed by the deliverances of conscience in the ordinary sense of the word. And assumptions with regard to conscience made in appraisal of the argument are subject to the same test. The claims made by Newman for conscience are inconsistent with those made by him for the authority of the

[2] Henri Bremond, *Newman: Essai de biographie psychologique* (Paris, 1906; 8th edn., 1932), 199.

Church, Bremond and others have maintained. And this might be true on one understanding of conscience and not on another; the important question will be whether it is true of conscience in the ordinary sense of the word, true of conscience in the ordinary conception of it.

An attempt is made in this essay to relate the notion of conscience in Newman's thought to features of conscience in the ordinary conception of it. But what is meant by the *ordinary* conception of conscience? What is to be taken as the criterion of ordinariness here? The phrase 'conscience in the ordinary sense of the word'—which we have replaced by 'conscience in the ordinary conception of it', since we are dealing with something wider in scope than the sense of a word—suggests an answer: the ordinary conception of conscience is the conception embodied in the idiomatic locutions of ordinary speech containing the word 'conscience'; more generally, it is the conception implicit in the way the word functions in ordinary speech. In the first chapter of the essay we shall be occupied with the content of this conception. Our immediate task is a fuller account of its general nature.

II

Little work has been done on the conception of conscience we are calling the ordinary conception. It was neglected even by the Ordinary-Language philosphers, though a single paper, Ryle's 'Conscience and Moral convictions' (1940), does a good deal to make up for the neglect. The very possibility that there might be any ordinary conception of conscience which might have to be distinguished from the conceptions which have operated in the theories of some philosophers goes unrecognized in the article on Conscience in *The Encyclopedia of Philosophy*[3] published in 1967, whose volumes are a compendium of the views and perspectives of contemporary English-speaking philosphers.

That it could be a *discovery* that the deliverances of one's

---

[3] *Encyclopedia of Philosophy,* ed. Paul Edwards (New York, 1967).

conscience relate only to one's own conduct shows the extent
to which, from the latitudinarian use of its name, something as
familiar to us as conscience can have its nature obscured. The
following quotation come from Ryle's paper 'Conscience and
Moral Convictions':

In discussing the conflict between Moral Sense theories of ethical
knowledge (or conviction) and intellectual theories . . . recently, I
struck a point which was new to me. I had always vaguely supposed
that 'Conscience' is ordinarily used to signify any sort of knowledge
or conviction about what is right and wrong. So that *any* verdict
about the rightness of wrongness either of a particular type of
conduct or of a particular piece of conduct could be called a verdict
of 'Conscience'. I had also supposed that 'conscience' was too vague
and equivocal a word to enjoy any definite syntax.

But then I noticed that 'conscience' is *not* used in this way. We
limit the verdicts of conscience to judgments about the rightness or
wrongness of the acts only of the owner of that conscience.[4]

There is much to be learnt from this passage about the
conception of conscience we are calling the ordinary conception of it. First, that there quite certainly is such a thing.

Obscuring the existence of this conception, fostering a
supposition to the effect that 'conscience' is too vague or
equivocal a word to enjoy any definite syntax, is the very
common freehand use of it, in which, in extreme cases, what is
conveyed is a feeling rather than a meaning, the word
retaining only its resonance. ('All that may be known of God is
revealed to heart and conscience.') Also obscuring the
existence of the ordinary-language conception of conscience
has been the use of the word 'conscience' by philosophers and
theologians as a term of theory. In its use as a term of theory
'conscience' has a more or less definite syntax, but one given to
it by its user, modifying in some degree the one it already has
in its ordinary use. An example of a theory-use of 'conscience'
is contained in the passage from Ryle: designating as 'a verdict
of conscience' *any* judgement on the rightness or wrongness of
conduct. However much it may be obscured, the existence of
the ordinary conception of conscience is made clearly evident
when a manner of speaking, authorized by some departure

---

[4] Gilbert Ryle, 'Conscience and Moral Convictions' (1940), in *Collected Papers*
(London, 1971), ii. 185.

from it, clashes with what can properly or naturally be said. Thus, if a judgement on the rightness or wrongness of no matter whose conduct was a judgement of one's conscience, according to the ordinary conception of conscience, it ought not to be outlandish to say such a thing as 'My conscience condemns what you are doing.'

Besides opening our eyes to the existence of a conception of conscience rightly describable as ordinary, the passage from Ryle, being a set of comments on the use of a word, helps to make us realize the way in which the conception exists. It exists implicitly in the use of the word 'conscience' in accordance with the conventions of ordinary speech; it has to be extracted from its linguistic setting if there is to be, for the most part, more than a vague and precarious awareness of its content.

We have proceeded very much as though there was only one conception of conscience entitled to be called ordinary. But there is another claimant to the title besides the one we have been describing. The conception of conscience held by most people ought surely to be called an ordinary conception of conscience, if not *the* ordinary conception of it. Of course it might be that the two conceptions happened to have the same content; that what most people think conscience is and does coincides with what it is and does in the ordinary-language conception of it. The two conceptions would not become a single one in virtue of this coincidence; their rationale is different. The content of the conception whose ordinariness might be described as statistical would be ascertained in the same way as the existence of this conception, by a polling of opinions on conscience. No other investigation would be needed, since, according to this conception, what conscience is and does is simply what most people would say it was and did. The content of the ordinary-language conception has to be worked out from the functioning of the word 'conscience' in ordinary speech.

It is the ordinary-language conception of conscience which is rightly describable as *the* ordinary conception of it. For anyone with an opinion about conscience assumes as a matter of course that it holds good of conscience 'in the ordinary sense of the word'. Who cares about what conscience is or does in some extended sense of the word?

Mistakes regarding some feature of the ordinary-language conception of conscience, from now on called without qualification the ordinary conception of conscience, are very possible and may be common. (Common enough, perhaps, to be included in what most people would say conscience is or does.) It is not possible for the conception of conscience implicit in the ordinary-language use of the word 'conscience' to be mistaken about conscience. Conscience is not like the brain or the heart, misconceptions about which can be removed by anatomical or physiological investigation. Conscience is like the 'heart' spoken of in the Bible. For the heart in the Biblical sense of the word (there may be more than one sense but we shall suppose one), there are the relevant Biblical passages; for conscience, there are the familiar locutions of everyday speech, such as 'a bad conscience', 'a good conscience', 'a matter of conscience', and more generally, the way the word functions in its ordinary use. It is not possible for the Biblical conception of the heart to be a misconception of it; there is no unitary original to which the conception can fail to correspond, nothing external to it, which is the heart. As with the heart, so with conscience. What conscience is or does is what it is or does in the ordinary conception of it. From now on we shall often speak indifferently of conscience in the ordinary conception of it, and of conscience.

Though it is not possible for the Biblical conception of the heart to be mistaken about the *heart*, or for the ordinary conception of conscience to be mistaken about *conscience*, there is nothing in the logic of the matter to prevent either conception from being mistaken about something external to itself. These conceptions single out aspects of human nature. There is no logical impediment to their incorporating mistakes about what is within the area they cover. The mistakes might be about some human tendency or capacity. Two other possibilities in the ordinary conception of conscience need to be remarked upon. (Corresponding remarks would be applicable to the Biblical conception of the heart.) There might be— there is no logical impediment to there being—some incoherence in the conception: locutions of impeccable ordinariness containing the word 'conscience' might have conflicting implications for the characterization of conscience at some point. The further possibility is that certain points in the characterization of conscience might have to remain undecided because the relevant linguistic material is too exiguous or its implications too shaky. On the matter of undecidability a remark is needed which applies to the whole enterprise of deriving a conception of conscience from the ordinary use of the word: the boundary between ordinary and unordinary is not knife-edged.

The linguistic material which can be turned to most account in an enquiry into the nature of conscience consists of locutions containing the word 'conscience' which are understood by everyone who has learnt to speak his native language. Having 'a bad conscience' is a notable example. We know clearly what a bad conscience is, however much might still have to be brought to light before we know with clarity what conscience is. The functioning of the word 'conscience' in its ordinary use is often not noticeable until something goes wrong, until the word is employed in some unnatural way. In contrast with what can be obtained from an investigation of locutions such as 'a bad conscience', the information about conscience made available when the word is used unnaturally is negative, though it might be very important: we are enabled to delete something from a characterization of conscience.

It needs to be emphasized that an enquiry into the nature of conscience could not be purely linguistic. The examination of the linguistic material constituting its primary data would obviously involve the enquirer in noticing various things about himself. Self-scrutiny by itself, however, could disclose nothing of the nature of conscience, because nothing observed could be identified as belonging to conscience—whether, for instance, one's conscience passes judgement on someone else's action, is a question settled by what can properly be said, not by introspection. And, of course, a conceptual enquiry into conscience is only that. For a 'real' as opposed to a merely 'notional' apprehension of the nature of conscience (to borrow Newman's terms), a phenomenological account of conscience is needed, of the kind given by Newman.

III

In the first chapter of this essay an attempt will be made to bring into view as much of the ordinary conception of conscience as is necessary for an understanding and appraisal of Newman's thought when the notion of conscience enters into it. It is a very impressionistic attempt, but since (to adapt a remark of Adam Smith's about moral philosophy) we are dealing here with the domestic affairs of that parish of which everyone is an inhabitant, the reader is able to check what is being said.

Besides attempting to relate Newman's conception of conscience to the ordinary conception of conscience, the essay has a more general concern. This is to give a comprehensive account of Newman's thought about conscience with particular attention to the difficulties in it, which are surprisingly frequent. Commentary on Newman's thought about conscience has tended to be celebratory rather than investigatory, and has shown an inadequate sense of the need to slow down at the difficulties. Different kinds of thing, of course, are liable to be seen as difficulties, accordingly as Newman is viewed from different perspectives—Scholastic, say, or Phenomenological, or that of the British tradition in philosophy (the perspective in this essay). And close attention to some of the things we shall be looking at has been hindered in important commentary by the placing of his conception of conscience in wide themes, such as 'the personal conquest of truth' according to Newman, and Newman's 'personnalisme moral'. This essay has a narrow enough theme to allow time to be spent on the difficulties.

These difficulties often contain a philosophical element. The essay is broadly philosophical in character, though conscience is a subject of more theological than philosophical interest. Its neglect by analytically-minded philosophers reflects a sense that exploration of it would yield little of philosophical value. Put at the centre of moral philosophy by Butler in the eighteenth century, the notion of conscience has been largely relegated to the history of moral philosophy (for reasons that will be touched upon later) by British philosophers in the twentieth century.

THE ORDINARY CONCEPTION
OF CONSCIENCE

THIS chapter is preparatory to our enquiry into Newman's thought about conscience. With features of his thought in mind, but for the most part with no reference to them, an attempt will be made to bring into view relevant features of the ordinary conception of conscience. This will be done mainly through a discussion of two questions: whether conscience ever determines right and wrong; how conscience is related in idea to oneself.

The first of these questions needs some immediate comment. It might be that the ordinary conception of conscience assigns to it a determination of right and wrong, but one restricted in various ways. With this possibility in mind, we want to know whether conscience ever determines right and wrong, or whether doing this lies altogether outside its province.

'Right' and 'wrong' are Newman's usual words in connection with conscience, 'right' having the force of 'required, obligatory'. It will have this force in our use of it. Newman assumed that moral rightness and wrongness are objective, there to be ascertained, not constituted by approvals and disapprovals or anything of the sort. To ask whether conscience ever determines right and wrong reflects this assumption. But we do not want to ask a question the answer to which might commit the ordinary conception of conscience to moral objectivism. Objectivist terms are hard to avoid when the categorizing of actions as right or wrong is under discussion, and neutral terms are liable to be unsatisfactory in other ways. We shall not avoid using expressions more strongly objectivist than 'determine', which has a certain ambiguity; we shall ask, for example, whether conscience is to be understood as a source of, or as imparting, moral knowledge. (And in no deviation from ordinary usage—'You must have known that that was wrong' is anybody's remark.) However variously expressed, the question whether the ordinary conception of conscience assigns to it any determination of right and wrong is to be understood as having an objectivist–subjectivist neutrality.

A further remark needs to be made about what will be meant by 'determine'. We want to be able to refer to categorizations of actions as right or wrong which are, or might be, mistaken. So the question whether conscience ever determines right and wrong is to be understood as asking whether it ever engages in the determination of right and wrong. We shall be taking incidental notice in this chapter of what conscience would have in the way of resources if in the ordinary conception of it it does engage in this enterprise. An autonomous operation is in question, conscience relying upon itself.

I

The formation of the word 'conscience' might be cautiously expected to throw some light on the conception implicit in the developed use of the word. 'Conscience', the *Oxford English Dictionary* states, is a word borrowed from the French, which replaced the earlier English word 'inwit', and is an adaptation of the Latin

conscientia privity of knowledge (with another), knowledge within oneself, consciousness, conscience . . . f. *con-* together + *scīre* to know; thus *conscīre alii* to know along with another, to be privy with another to a matter, thence, *conscīre sibi* to know with oneself only, to know within one's own mind.

The knowledge shared with another, or with others, might be of various sorts of things. It was, however, often of plots and crimes—guilty knowledge. And when the knowledge is of some wrongdoing of one's own, and the other—a witness and an accuser—with whom the knowledge is shared[1] is oneself, the idea is present in accordance with which the word *conscientia*, when used absolutely, strongly suggested a bad conscience. The *Thesaurus Linguae Latinae* has a quotation which interestingly shows *conscientia*, meaning conscience, in relation to, and in contrast with, a word prominent in the group from which *conscientia* emerges with this meaning: 'vos conscios timetis, nos etiam conscientiam solam'—'you are afraid of others knowing; we fear only conscience'.

Various sorts of things could be 'known within one's own mind'; there could be in a person, for example, *conscientia* of his lost fortune, of his good will towards someone, of his duty. There was also the *conscientia boni aut mali facti*; and here inward consciousness and conscience meet. The knowledge within one's own mind was not a bare, indifferent cognition; the *conscientia* of whatever it was was a sense or feeling of it. But while the *mala conscientia* was just what a bad conscience is with us, the *bona conscientia*, in typical descriptions of it, was more than merely the absence of any consciousness of wrongdoing and its attendant sense of guilt, which is all that a good conscience seems to be with us. A good conscience is like good health, which you have when you are not in bad or indifferent health. The *bona conscientia* was, typically, a sense of self-approval.

Until a surprisingly recent date the English word 'conscience' could be used like *conscientia* (and like the French *conscience*, the German *Gewissen*, the Italian *coscienza)* to mean either conscience or consciousness. The following quotation in the *Oxford English Dictionary* comes from a source as late as 1869: 'The conscience of this sharpens and exasperates the temper of his will.' From Swift's sermon on the 'Testimony of Conscience' (before 1745) the *Dictionary* quotes this sentence: 'The word Conscience properly signifies, that knowledge which a man hath within himself of his own thoughts and actions.' This is not in fact what the word meant when it

---

[1] The 'other' in later centuries of the Christian era was sometimes thought of as God, as in the following quotation, which calls up these primitive associations of the idea of conscience: 'The notation of ye word Con-scientia, denotes a kind of combination . . . betwene two in the knowledge of some secreate, & this is betweene God and ye soule of man.' This comes from some notes on conscience made by John Donne. See 'A Donne Discovery', *Times Literary Supplement*, 16 Aug. 1974.

meant conscience (as the sermon itself incidentally shows by being unable to confine it to its 'proper' signification).

Swift is a warning. Nevertheless, it would be what the formation of the word points to if it is found that conscience restricts itself to that of which one is inwardly conscious. It would be in line, therefore, with etymological considerations if, to anticipate a conclusion of this chapter, it should turn out that determining right and wrong is not something conscience does. On an objectivist view of right and wrong, this would not be something that conscience could do if restricted to cognizance of that of which one is inwardly conscious. We are inwardly conscious of feelings and states of mind. An objective rightness or wrongness is one existing independently of any feelings or states of mind an action might induce in us.

As compared with its state 150 years or so earlier, the notion of conscience had undergone by Newman's time great expansion and elevation, in the use made of it by writers. Encrustation covered the ordinary conception. Extracts from two dictionary entries under the heading 'Conscience' provide an instructive contrast. The first is from Dr Johnson's *Dictionary* (1755). Conscience is 'The knowledge or faculty by which we judge of the goodness or wickedness of ourselves.' The other comes from the *Oxford English Dictionary*: 'Opinions as to the nature, function, and authority of conscience are widely divergent, varying from the conception of the mere exercise of the ordinary judgement on moral questions, to that of an infallible guide of conduct, a sort of deity within us.' In a statement prior to this summary of opinions, conscience is 'the faculty or principle which pronounces on the moral quality of one's actions and motives, approving the right and condemning the wrong'. But the first of the two conceptions between which the range of opinion on conscience is said to lie—that of conscience as being the exercise of ordinary judgement on moral questions—brings in the whole impersonal field of 'moral questions', and leaves out mention of judgement upon oneself which, in the quotation from Johnson's *Dictionary*, is the business of conscience. And while the conduct referred to in the statement of the second conception is presumably one's own, the conscience superintending it has lost all ordinariness. The extent to which what is distinctive of conscience can fail to be reflected even in a widely held idea of conscience is suggested by the *Oxford Dictionary's* remark: 'Popularly the word is often used for the whole moral nature.'

II

Does conscience ever determine right and wrong? As remarked just now, it would be in line with etymological considerations if it does not; but no more value, of course, than that of a preliminary indication can be allowed to an etymologically derived limit on what is to be correctly ascribed to conscience. During the course of time the content of the ordinary conception of conscience, the conception implicit in the ordinary use of the word, might have been enlarged well beyond what the formation of the word would indicate, some extended use of it having become ordinary. A notable enlargement of this conception has historically taken place. To the original accusatory or condemnatory operation of conscience regarding an action done has been added the imperatival operation it now also has, that of commanding or prohibiting an action contemplated.

Well, then, does conscience, in the ordinary conception of it, ever determine what it commands or prohibits? Is it a source of moral knowledge in this conception? Or, to express the question differently yet again—since the repetition of a formula might deaden sensibility to what would answer the question—does conscience in this conception of it ever autonomously pronounce actions right or wrong?

Consider the refusal to take part in something on grounds of conscience. A nurse refuses to take part in an abortion, for example, because, she says, to do so is against her conscience or prohibited by her conscience. Saying this, in any one of the verbal forms in which it might be said, she renders herself liable as a matter of logic, as a consequence of the way the word 'conscience' functions when thus employed, to being asked *why* doing this is against her conscience. What this fact strongly indicates is that conscience is not a source of convictions on right and wrong: the very assertion that such-and-such is against one's conscience implicitly points away from one's conscience when the question why something is believed to be right or wrong comes up.

To return to the specific case, how might the nurse answer when asked why taking part in an abortion is against her conscience? Might she say: 'It just is'? So far from bringing before our minds with this answer any notion of conscience as a self-authenticating source of moral knowledge, she could not say anything feebler. An answer that she might give is that it is against her conscience to take part in an abortion because abortion is murder. We shall not monitor any of the discussion that might then ensue; if it took its natural path there would be no occasion for any further mention of conscience.

No one would say, would he, except as a joke, that murder was against his conscience? A person would not make that remark nor would it be made of him, seriously, about anything that comes under platitudinous moral condemnation. Perhaps this has nothing to do with conscience and only reflects the peculiarity of a solemn assertion of the obvious. Have him say, then, something that is not obvious: that he knows from his conscience that murder is wrong. The peculiarity of that remark certainly has to do with conscience. And one source of its peculiarity would lie in the fact that, embedded in the notion of conscience, as we shall observe later on, is the notion of conflict, which does not open up over the platitudinous.

Suppose it not to be part of the business of conscience to inform us of such truths as that murder, cruelty, and lying are wrong (truths without an acknowledgement of which society could not hold together). It may yet be the case, for all that the limited enquiry we are now engaged in could show, that such knowledge is obtained in just the way it would be if conscience were its source—that is, without reasoning, with the immediacy of feeling, as if it were by sense. For that is the manner in which conscience works. An opinion among philosophers has been that whatever reasoning can accomplish once we are in possession of moral principles, it is unable to put us in possession of these. They have to be ascertained by some mode of direct apprehension. Effected by what instrumentality? Conscience was there, did not have to be postulated; its manner of working was of the right sort: how easy to ascribe to conscience the direct apprehension of moral principles. At the opposite end of the scale from moral principles are actions in their fully determinate circumstances, their rightness or wrongness needing in this particularity to be discerned, it might seem, by something akin to sense perception: how easy to ascribe this discernment to conscience, which in its superintendence of conduct commands or prohibits particular actions.

Nothing is explained when any determination of right and wrong is ascribed to conscience. If conscience ever determines right and wrong, it delivers its finding oracularly. 'My conscience tells me this is wrong because . . .' is not something we would say. Apart from any other impediment to saying it, the reference to conscience would be pointless: if we are able to say that the thing is wrong for such-and-such a reason, we do not need to be informed that it is wrong. Nothing is illuminated when conscience is thought of as determining right and wrong, and a commonplace of moral discourse is obscured—the asking for and the giving of reasons when actions are asserted to be right or wrong.[2]

There is a telling done by conscience that is not in question. It is an admonitory telling, as contrasted with an informative one. It is aimed at deterrence, or conversely, at bringing about the performance of an action. And as admonition often does, it makes use of what is already known: a person is told by his conscience not to do something he knows (or suspects) to be wrong, or to do what he acknowledges (or would acknowledge if he was honest with himself) to be required of him. We shall look again at this act of conscience further on in the chapter. Mention of it now will assist the elucidation of a passage we are about to consider, and it enables us to make plainer by means of a contrast the question we have been asking in various ways: whether conscience ever *originates* knowledge of right and wrong, as contrasted with activating a knowledge already possessed.

A famous passage from Butler shows how unobtrusively a

[2] This double consideration would go a long way towards accounting for the relegation in effect of the notion of conscience to the history of moral philosophy, by British philosophers in the 20th cent.

theory of moral knowledge according to which right and wrong are apprehended non-inferentially, intuitively, can be expressed in the course of a description of conscience. We shall reproduce the whole passage because of the partial anticipation at its end of what Newman would make so much of:

> there is a superior principle of reflection or conscience in every man, which distinguishes between the internal principles of his heart, as well as his external actions: which passes judgment upon himself and them; pronounces determinately some actions to be in themselves just, right, good; others to be in themselves evil, wrong, unjust: which without being consulted, without being advised with, magisterially exerts itself, and approves or condemns him the doer of them accordingly: and which, if not forcibly stopped, naturally and always of course goes on to anticipate a higher and more effectual sentence, which shall hereafter second and affirm its own.[3]

Where is the intrusion of moral theory into this description of the operations of conscience? It is where Butler says that conscience 'pronounces determinately some actions to be in themselves just, right, good; others to be in themselves evil, wrong, unjust'—given two things: first, that it is not part of the ordinary conception of conscience that conscience ever originates the conviction that an action is right or wrong; secondly, that the slightly ambiguous word 'pronounces' does assign this originative role to conscience, the pronouncing of actions 'just, right, good' or the opposite being not merely admonitory but informative.

Resuming the question whether conscience, in the ordinary conception of it, ever originates the conviction that an action is right or wrong, let us recall what Ryle reported himself as having noticed regarding the use of the word 'conscience': 'We

---

[3] Joseph Butler, *Sermons* (1726), No. 2, in *Butler's Works*, ed. Gladstone (Oxford, 1896), ii. 59. By a 'principle of reflection' Butler means a power of self-reflexivity, a power to bring before ourselves the motives of our actions, our moral state generally. It is not implied, then, by this designation of conscience that when conscience 'pronounces' actions right or wrong, it does so only after a process of what we would understand by 'reflection', into which reasoning might enter. These is nothing in the designation of conscience as a principle of reflection in any degree running counter to the moral intuitionism usually attributed to Butler. In view of Butler's great significance for Newman (see *Apologia*, ch. 1, pp. 10–11), there are surprisingly few traces of his account of conscience in Newman's account of it. There are, of course, some considerable similarities in the content of both.

limit the verdicts of conscience to judgments about the
rightness or wrongness of the acts only of the owner of that
conscience.⁴ There is perhaps some ambiguity in this statement; at any rate there is an important distinction to be made.
To be distinguished are: (1) a judgement of blameworthiness
or blamelessness on a person by his conscience in respect of an
act of his; (2) the judgement of a person's conscience that an
act he is contemplating is right or wrong—more complicatedly,
that it would be right or wrong for him. Now a good reason
why one's conscience does not deliver judgements of the first
kind, a condemnatory judgement, say, on someone else,
would be that I can look into myself as I cannot look into you,
and it might be that what I find inexcusable in myself would
be excusable in you. But if one's conscience delivers judgements
of the right-and-wrong determining sort at all, their being
limited to one's own acts is altogether surprising. Suppose my
conscience to deliver the straightforward judgement: This act
would be wrong. That judgement ought to be as applicable to
you as to me. Suppose, more complicatedly, my conscience to
judge that my doing the thing would be wrong. Implied is a
reference to the special character of my circumstances. This
judgement, however, is very easily rendered impersonal
because it is implicitly universal. If it would be wrong for me
to do whatever it is, it would be wrong for anyone to do it—
anyone whose circumstances are not relevantly different
from mine.

But the fact is that my conscience cannot deliver judgements
of any kind on the conduct of others—not on the rightness or
wrongness of what they are doing any more than on their
justifiability or culpability in doing it. I can pass these
judgements of course on the conduct of others; the conceptually
circumscribed 'part' of myself which is my conscience cannot.

Our tentative conclusion is that there is no determination of
right and wrong by conscience, in the ordinary conception of
it. When something is asserted to be against, or required by,
one's conscience, a reason is implied, and it is not produced by
one's conscience; conscience points away from itself. If
conscience ever determines right and wrong, it ought, at least
sometimes, to be in order to speak of one's conscience as

⁴ 'Conscience and Moral Convictions', p. 185.

judging the actions of someone else to be right or wrong; and it never is. In section IV of this chapter we shall look at representatives of a class of familiar locutions which, considered in abstraction from the circumstances of their ordinary use, could seem to have implications inconsistent with the conclusion we have reached. Their existence helps to explain what is something of a puzzle if conscience does not determine right and wrong: its being widely supposed that it does.

The resources conscience would have for this undertaking are meagre. It would have to effect its determination of right and wrong, no matter how complicated the case, in a divinatory manner, for it does not engage in reasoning. The evidence that conscience does not engage in reasoning is evidence of the same kind as establishes that its declarations on conduct are restricted to one's own conduct: the contrary supposition involves manifest departure from what ordinary language allows us to say. We can count on never hearing anyone say that his conscience makes inferences, goes into various considerations, reaches conclusions, thinks anything out.

III

To explain why the declarations of one's conscience relate only to one's own conduct is the main undertaking of Ryle's paper. Discussion of the explanation he puts forward will take us to where we can see that the concern of one's conscience with one's own conduct, is necessarily with it in its particularity.

To be really convinced by any rule of conduct (a rule of etiquette, for example, a rule of prudence, or a moral rule) is to be disposed, Ryle argues, to behave in accordance with the rule, the behaviour being understood to include thinking and speaking in accordance with the rule. My moral convictions really or—to use Ryle's word—'operatively' held thus necessarily influence my actions in a way that they necessarily cannot influence the actions of someone else. Thus held they are my conscience, Ryle says:

Conscience is not something other than, prior to or posterior to moral convictions; it is having those convictions in an operative degree, i.e. being disposed to behave acordingly. And it is active or calls for attention when this disposition is baulked by some contrary inclination. Conscience has nothing to say when the really honest man is asked a question and when he has no temptation to deceive. He then tells the truth as he signs his name, without considering what to do or why he should do it or how to get himself to do it . . . Pangs or qualms of conscience can occur only when I am both disposed to act in one way and disposed to act in another and when one of these dispositions is an operative moral principle. ('Conscience and Moral Convictions', p. 189)

It is clear on Ryle's account of conscience why my conscience cannot operatively direct someone else's behaviour: a behavioral disposition of mine is not another's. And on Ryle's account of conscience the impossibility of our saying something like 'My conscience forbids you to do this, requires you to do that' will have its explanation, one supposes, in that the imperative 'speech' of conscience, verbalized into a statement of command or prohibition, will express the disposition to act in accordance with one's moral conviction when the actualizing of this disposition is being impeded. When my conscience thus speaks it will therefore necessarily confine its address to me.

An ingenious explanation of the restriction of the *imper-atival* declarations of one's conscience to oneself has been provided, but no light is thrown on our restricting all 'verdicts' of conscience in such a way, if these include judgements as to the rightness or wrongness of actions. In the passage from Ryle which is before us, conscience is not represented as making judgements of any kind. In this passage conscience is the having of moral convictions 'in an operative degree'. In the earlier passage from Ryle, however, judgements that an action is right or wrong are, or strongly appear to be, attributed to conscience. ('We limit the verdicts of conscience to judgments about the rightness or wrongness of the acts only of the owner of that conscience.') If conscience makes such judgements at all, it was argued just now, they cannot be limited to the actions of the owner of the conscience. And since one's conscience cannot pronounce on the conduct of others, the conclusion was drawn that conscience makes no judgements as to the rightness or wrongness of actions. If it makes no judgements of this kind, then obviously there is no limitation on their range needing to be explained.

Ryle's account of conscience does not explain a type of declaration which indisputably does proceed from conscience. If conscience forces itself on our notice only when tendencies to action are in conflict, its condemnation can be felt before, during, and residually, just after an action done against moral conviction; but not long after, not years later, when conscience with no opposition to overcome has lapsed back into its merely dispositional being. There is division of a kind within me, I am not at one with myself, when I feel pangs of conscience about something I did, but nothing occurs which is analoguous to being 'disposed to act in one way and disposed to act in another'. Since my conscience can condemn me for a past action, it has an utterance which is not to be accounted for as manifesting a conflict of behavioural tendencies within me. Its always addressing itself only to oneself is, therefore, not to be explained on that basis.

How is this fact to be explained? My conscience cannot condemn me for what you did, and your conscience cannot order me to do this and forbid me to do that. Why not? No explanation can be asked for my not condemning myself for what I did not do but you did, and self-addressed imperatives cannot come to me from someone else. What, then, has to be explained? Nothing except the ascription of self-condemnation and self-addressed imperatives of a certain kind to conscience, and this is a matter of the history of a word, a word which once meant both consciousness and conscience, derived from a word whose formation suggests that what conscience will have before it is only that of which one is inwardly conscious.

Let us now consider Ryle's description of what observably occasions an imperatival operation of conscience. Presupposed in the situation as he describes it are already existing moral convictions. No judgement as to rightness or wrongness has to be made. Nothing has to be ascertained. Among a person's moral convictions is the conviction that lying is wrong. And what brings his conscience into operation is that instead of telling the truth as a matter of course, he is tempted to lie. We have here an example of the situation in relation to which conscience is figuratively endowed with powers of speech, in the direction of conduct. It is in a situation of this kind that 'the voice of conscience' is heard, to cite the commonest of the conscience speech-metaphors. Our interest is in the content of these utterances.

Now, it cannot be that in the precise case before us, conscience is announcing to a person anything it has determined, saying to him, as it were, 'The action you are contemplating is not right'. The right thing to do was already known; nothing had to be determined. Conscience is speaking imperativally, commanding that something taken as a matter of course to be right, be *done*.

Suppose now a case in which the rightness or wrongness of the action commanded or prohibited by conscience was not able to be taken for granted. And suppose, contrary to the stong indications we have observed, that there is a determination of rightness and wrongness proper to conscience; specifically, that it is for it to determine the rightness or wrongness of what it commands or prohibits. This act of conscience would not be reflected in the conduct-directing utterances of conscience we are considering. The reason is that any determination of right and wrong that might be necessary occurs antecedently to the situation in which they are appropriately attributed to conscience. Characterizing this situation is a reluctance to do or abstain from something whose rightness or wrongness has been taken for granted, or decided upon.

There are, however, no grounds for the supposition that when we have to act in one way or another, and the right thing to do has to be determined, it is for conscience to determine it. What happens has to be described in terms of what is undertaken by a person not by his conscience. He tries to work out what ought to be done making use of ratiocinative procedures conscience does not possess, in the ordinary conception of it, and does not need for its own operations. And it might be that he does not want to do the thing he settles on as right. Then, just as when there was no question as to what was right, his conscience comes on the scene; and not until then, provided he made an honest attempt—so far as self-awareness can discern—to work out what ought to be done. If the attempt was less than honest, a sensitive conscience will have had an earlier utterance, this time an accusatory one.

The commands and prohibitions of conscience are not general commands and prohibitions. In the example of the coming of conscience into operation, which we have been discussing, it would be inappropriate to imagine conscience as issuing a general prohibition against lying. The voice of conscience is not heard otherwise than as requiring, against reluctance or desire, that this thing, in these circumstances, be done or avoided. Urging us imperatively against reluctance or desire to do or turn away from the thing we are contemplating, conscience directs our conduct in a manner that is necessarily particular.

Reluctant to do what he sees as right, wanting to do what he sees as wrong, a person is in conflict with himself. Where there is no conflict, the notion of conscience is out of place. Ryle's paper brings this fact to our attention. Attention can be drawn by way of further comment on Ryle to how variously the ordinary conception of conscience incorporates the notion of conflict.

The passage from Ryle which we have been discussing contains an identification of one's conscience with the totality of one's moral convictions: 'Conscience is not something other than, prior to or posterior to moral convictions; it is having those convictions in an operative degree, i.e. being disposed to behave accordingly.'[5] It is strange to find Ryle identifying conscience with the possession of moral convictions, and an indication of how easy it is to lose one's way when talking about conscience. That a person's moral convictions are his conscience is the very supposition Ryle mentions at the beginning of his paper, and goes on to reject: 'I had always vaguely supposed that "Conscience" is ordinarily used to signify any sort of knowledge or conviction about what is right and wrong' (p. 185). One took him to have rejected this supposition on the ground that if a person's moral convictions are his conscience, it ought to be quite in order for one person's conscience to deliver verdicts on another person's actions. Our concern now is with a different point. An

---

[5] The convictions on which there is a disposition to act are not a special class of moral convictions. Due in a measure to Ryle's influence, it has become a well-founded philosophical commonplace that a disposition to behave in accordance with the conviction enters into the notion of having a moral conviction.

ordinary use of the word 'conscience' in which the word signified the totality of one's moral convictions would be at odds with the conflict-element in the notion of conscience. If a moral conviction of mine is called my *conscience,* it is picked out from my other moral convictions as a conviction I am going against, or which I am tempted to go against; or, on the contrary, it is a conviction I am acting upon, but it is at odds with what others think right. In his exploratory paper Ryle saw, but did not keep steadily in mind, that the notion of conflict is embedded in the ordinary conception of conscience, so that where all conflict is absent this conception is misapplied. The conflict may be within a person. There is something he believes he ought or ought not to do, and to act accordingly he has to overcome resistance within himself: he experiences the imperative of conscience. His conscience condemns him for something he did or left undone: he is divided against himself in self-condemnation.

The conflict may, however, not be within a person, but between him and others, and it may only be anticipated. If something is a matter of conscience for anyone, he expects opposition if this is not already actual. A person's conscience makes him bold in facing opposition because its imperative confronts him, if its imperative is needed, with whatever it is as something he must or must not do. When anyone is said to be mistaken in conscience, some conviction of his is referred to as his conscience. No dissonance within him is implied; the conflict implied is one of conviction between him and the speaker. The person of whom it is said that he is acting according to his conscience is not acting according to some platitudinous moral conviction; it is not, for instance, said of someone who is tempted to lie but is not lying, that he is acting according to his conscience; if this is said of someone, the conviction according to which he is acting must be, or seem likely to be, called in question.

IV

There is a class of familiar locutions containing the word 'conscience' which might seem to imply, against the strong indications we have noticed, that there is a determination of right and wrong proper to conscience. It is an appearance these locutions have when looked at in abstraction from circumstances appropriate to their use. What is to be made of the injunction 'Always be guided by your conscience'? Let us imagine a situation in which it might have been given—to a young man leaving home and going out into the world. (It is not an injunction with a highly contemporary ring.) What is being enjoined upon him? Not that he should look within himself for direction when he is puzzled as to the right thing to do. Given with morally dubious situations in mind, it is an injunction to him not to let pressure or inclination have him *do* what he suspects is wrong. It does not pronounce at all on the manner in which right conduct is to be ascertained. In particular, it carries no implication that conscience is a guide in perplexity. You would be teasing someone manifestly genuine in his perplexity by asking him why he did not consult his conscience. That question would be appropriate only if he was thought to be hiding something from himself. My conscience can prompt the question 'What ought I to do?'; it can impel me to set about answering it; it does not undertake to answer it. To anticipate a general conclusion: conscience effects doing, not knowing.

Our conscience 'tells' us that an action we are contemplating is wrong. But what we are told we already know, or suspect. This telling is not a conveying of information: it is admonitory; it presupposes the knowledge, or suspicion, that it might conceivably look as though it generated. Under what circumstances could it appropriately be said to someone 'Your conscience must have told you that that was wrong'? Under the circumstances in which it could have been said, alternatively, 'You knew very well that that was wrong.' A person can tell himself—alternatively, his conscience can be said to tell him—that what he is contemplating is, say, adultery. No information is being conveyed. And none when he tells himself with prohibitatory repetitiveness (condemnation being already implied by 'adultery') that adultery is wrong.

Consider the expression 'an awakened conscience'. It is an expression which reflects both of the great roles assigned to conscience in the ordinary conception of it: its imperatival role—its role in the direction of conduct—and its accusatory or condemnatory role. There happens to be a painting which illustrates one of a variety of applications this expression can be given, the pre-Raphaelite work entitled *The Awakened Conscience*. In this painting a girl is on her feet, 'her wide eyes straining on vacancy as if seeing Hell open'; her seducer, one arm around her, is at the piano. Now, it is out of the question, of course, that the girl has just been told by her conscience, as though it was news, that what she has been doing was wrong; with her upbringing, she could not possibly not have known. But realization has set in and with it, or rather as part of it, the pangs of conscience. The expressions in the group of which 'an awakened conscience' is a member characterize a sudden or gradual, more or less intense realization of what one has done; or, looking to the future, a realization of the way one has been living, of changes required in one's conduct. One becomes aware of, so as to be affected by, what is already known dimly, or clearly but with indifference.

Conscience, as represented in the various ways of speaking in which it is figured as commanding, prohibiting, or as giving directions, addresses itself to the will. The adjective, 'conscientious' strongly intimates how these ways of speaking are to be understood. A conscientious person is one who is very ready to do, and who meticulously does, whatever seems to him to be incumbent upon him. He also goes to trouble to find out what is incumbent upon him. Being conscientious has to do with doing, not knowing. And conscience, presupposing knowledge, or suspicion, as to the character of an action, is concerned with having it done or avoided and, as we are about to notice briefly, with the agent.

Our conclusion on the issue which has been our main concern in this chapter is that the ordinary conception of conscience does not assign to it any determination of right and wrong. Such evidence as we have looked at might have pointed to incoherence in this conception, the negative indications which we first noticed colliding with what is to be read off from everyday locutions which have conscience directing conduct. But this has not happened. As directing conduct, conscience is to be viewed as urging us towards or away from an action whose rightness or wrongness is either taken for granted, or determined—but not by conscience—to be one or the other; and as urging us not to give the benefit of the doubt to the dubious.

V

Conscience, Newman said, is 'more than a man's own self'. His meaning will be discussed in a later chapter; he was in no way countenancing the idea which his words could fit, that conscience has a hidden being, is some entity within us with an agency of its own, of which the phenomena of conscience are manifestations. This idea is quite strongly suggested by a very familiar figure in the rhetoric of conscience, which is not absent from Newman's pages: the 'inward mentor', the 'secret monitor'. (The importance of ideas about conscience is that they tend to have practical consequences. This one further impedes recognition of the moral fact, already obscured by the phenomenological externality of the action of conscience— the way it forces itself upon us—that we are in large measure responsible for our conscience.) To take up the question whether conscience has a trans-phenomenal being and agency is at the same time to consider the relation between one's conscience and one's self.

A judicial office has been assigned to conscience by moralists, in which conscience pronounces upon oneself in respect of some action done or left undone. It pronounces acquittal or condemnation, sometimes it is said to pronounce commendation. There is artificiality in this judicial office constructed from the material supplied by expressions of ordinary language and the phenomena associated with them. And, against the intentions behind its construction, putting conscience into this office has some considerable appearance of putting into it a hanging judge. Conspicious in ordinary ways of speaking of conscience is its condemnatory or accusatory role. Accusatory, condemnatory—they do not seem to be two different roles; the circumstances in which a person is spoken of as 'accused' by his conscience or 'condemned' by it are, at the least, not clearly different. To this role (or these roles) belongs the punitive imagery of conscience—the pangs and the stabbing. Contrasted with the condemnatory or accusatory conscience is the good or the quiet conscience, between which, again, the difference, if any, is elusive. If a good conscience is the same as a quiet conscience or nearly so, there will not be characteristic psychological phenomena in which it manifests itself. Its presence will be normally accompanied by the absence of the phenomena of a bad, accusatory, condemnatory, active conscience. In general, conscience is disqualified for a cool, judicial office by the peremptoriness of its operations. Conscience delivers verdicts but conducts no judicial process.

Suppose the question arises for a person as to the disposition with which he has acted. The work he does to determine its integrity or otherwise is not, in an ordinary way of speaking, ascribed to his conscience, but just to him. He ends his self-examination, we shall suppose, satisfied—with a quiet conscience. Here an answer is indicated to the question whether conscience is some entity within us: the personification of conscience is not carried through; conscience lapses into identity with the person whose conscience it is. When the reifying metaphors in ordinary ways of speaking of conscience are pressed, their insubstantiality is disclosed.

A locution which throws light (in its first-person use) on the relation between one's conscience and oneself is 'an over-active conscience'. Someone with an over-active conscience is someone who works unremittingly at doing what he thinks he ought to, and is nagged at by his conscience all the time for not doing enough. There is a striking reversal of familiar roles as between a person and his conscience when he comes to admit that his conscience is over-active. Normally a person's conscience passes judgement on him; in calling his conscience over-active, he passes judgement on it. A natural paraphrase of this condemnation would be that he is letting mere feeling rule him, feeling with no rational justification, a paraphrase which tells against an entitative notion of conscience.

But what he condemns as over-active is not his conscience, it might be said, but his 'conscience'. Certainly, the word is liable to go into inverted commas in this case. And what makes the difference between conscience and 'conscience' here tells very hard against an entitative notion of conscience; for this difference turns entirely on how the person regards the situation. If he does not regard the nagging as justified, his feelings have no sanction. Without his ratification of them, it is merely psychological distress he is suffering; with it, condemnation by his conscience.

The rule that entities are not to be multiplied beyond necessity applies even when the question is whether ways of speaking have entitative implications. The phenomena of a conscience commanding or prohibiting, and of a conscience from which accusation or condemnation is proceeding, are feelings and more complex states of mind. No entity within us experiences these. Their only subject is obviously the person whose conscience is at work. Besides the phenomena, there is their ratification, deliberate or implicit, which makes them phenomena of conscience. All the entitative space is engrossed by the person experiencing and ratifying them; there is no *thing* left for conscience to be. A further consideration might be mentioned against seeing entitative implications in the references to conscience of ordinary speech: that there are dictates of prudence and of the heart, as well as of conscience; that prudence can restrain or require something of us, and the heart move us or hold us back. Prudence and the heart are thing only in metaphor. So is conscience.

Points brought up in this section have a bearing upon themes in Newman's thought about conscience which are considered in Chapter 3 of the essay; specifically, upon the mode of being he takes conscience to possess, and upon the transition he conducts from the phenomena of conscience to God. In deviation from the ordinary conception of conscience —if the conclusion we reached is correct—there is a determination of right and wrong belonging to conscience, in Newman's conception of it. Newman has conscience determine the rightness or wrongness of one's own contemplated actions. How he sees conscience as obtaining its result especially requires discussion. This is entered upon in the following chapter. The implications for his view of the relation between conscience and the authority of the Church, if any determination of right and wrong at all belongs to conscience, are discussed in Chapter 4.

2

'A MORAL SENSE'

ALL through Newman's writing there are remarks about conscience, and in various places he dwells on some feature of conscience. His most extensive, though still very brief, treatment of its nature comes in the *Grammar of Assent*, published in 1870. He enters on the subject there incidentally, in order to show how realization that there is a God is possible, as contrasted with a merely 'notional assent' to the proposition that God exists; and at the same time in order to show where a 'proof' of this proposition is to be looked for. There is a point which ought to be discussed now, before we come to the main topic of this chapter, so that we will not be bothered by it then. It is occasioned by Newman's speaking of conscience in two very different ways. He speaks of it in a way that implies that it acts or delivers dictates, and he speaks of it as an act, a dictate, a feeling ('this feeling of a law . . . which I call Conscience'). The second way of speaking occurs noticeably when the context is theoretical. This consideration, combined with Newman's intense metaphysical particularism—'the real is the particular'[1]—suggests that in his view conscience, so far as it is differentiated from oneself, is to be resolved into what are customarily referred to as its acts and states. We shall look briefly here at some of the textual grounds for attributing this view to him—in doing so, we shall see more clearly what it maintains with regard to conscience—and then answer the question whether it is a view with a bearing on anything else in his thought.

Newman associates conscience with memory and reason in the *Grammar of Assent*, making the point that it is as much an original endowment of our nature as they are. At the same time, what seem to be deliberately chosen words imply that it

[1] *Grammar of Assent*, ch. 5, § 2, p. 139.

does not have the same manner of being as they do. Earlier, not only had memory and reasoning been distinguished as 'faculties' from the acts from which their existence is inferred, but it was clearly implied that they are genuine *instrument-alities*, like the apparatus of breathing: 'We know indeed that we have a faculty by which we remember, as we know we have a faculty by which we breathe; but we gain this knowledge by abstraction or inference from its particular acts, not by direct experience.' (*Grammar of Assent*, ch. 4, § 1, p. 61) When conscience is later associated with memory and reason, it is not as a faculty; it is placed among 'our mental acts', along with the 'action' of memory and reasoning (ch. 5, § 1, p. 105).

Faculties lose all ontological significance in an essay, 'Revelation in its Relation to Faith', written near the end of Newman's life. There is some uncertainty in the language of the section of the essay which deals with the nature of faculties. A faculty is said to be 'the exercise of a power of the mind itself', having just previously been said to be, not the exercise of a power, but a power: faculties are not 'real and substantive'; 'they are no more than simple powers'. There is, however, no uncertainty in the language of the title to this section of the essay, which is 'On the Mind's Faculties existing, not "re," but "ratione," and therefore only abstract names for its operations'.[2] Memory and reason are now what conscience was in the *Grammar of Assent*, a class of the operations of the mind.

Nothing else in Newman's thought is affected by a resolution of conscience into a class of our mental acts and states. In particular, the doctrine that conscience is 'a simple element in our nature', 'a constituent element of the mind' is unaffected; for these expressions are not intended to designate an agency; their import is that conscience is underivable from anything else in the constitution of the mind and as little the product of our upbringing as reasoning and remembering are. Nor is this resolution of conscience into certain of our mental acts and states at odds with speaking of conscience as acting and as issuing dictates, instead of speaking of it as an act and a dictate. If the considerations mentioned near the end of the

---

[2] *Stray Essays* (privately printed, 1890; not included in the collected edn. of Newman's *Works*), pp. 100–3.

previous chapter are recalled, it will be seen that the reifying of conscience in ordinary language is no more than a way of speaking, with no ontological commitments running counter to the manner of being ascribed by Newman to conscience.

We can now begin discussion of the main topic in this chapter: how Newman took conscience to effect the determination of right and wrong it has in his conception of it.

I

Newman ascribes to conscience (to 'the feeling of conscience') a double aspect:

The feeling of conscience . . . is twofold:—it is a moral sense, and a sense of duty, a judgment of the reason and a magisterial dictate. Of course its act is indivisible; still it has these two aspects, distinct from each other, and admitting of a separate consideration. (*Grammar of Assent*, ch. 5, § 1, pp. 105–6)

Commenting on the term he has applied to the first of the two aspects he has distinguished in conscience, Newman remarks that while everyone 'knows what is meant by a good or bad conscience', 'Half the world would be puzzled to know what was meant by the moral sense' (p. 106). The remark is itself puzzling, in its implied identification of conscience as 'a magisterial dictate' with a good or bad conscience. This identification will be discussed at the beginning of the next chapter. Our concern at present is with what is meant when conscience is called by Newman a moral sense. This concern is not with a mere exegetical nicety. As a moral sense, conscience is to determine right and wrong in the actual situations in which we find ourselves. At issue is Newman's conception of the way in which conscience accomplishes this determination. In the background is a question as to the reliability of conscience in guiding our path.

As used in the *Grammar of Assent*, the term 'moral sense' clearly reflects something of its philosophical history. A glance at this will make evident a good deal that is important for an understanding of Newman's notion of a moral sense.

In the eighteenth century one of a cluster of 'sense' expressions, such as 'a sense of the ridiculous', 'a sense of honour', 'a sense of beauty', became a term of theory—'moral sense'. Moral-sense theory was of two types. According to the predominant type, the moral sense (as described by Hume[3]) is 'a pleasure or uneasiness of a particular kind' induced by the contemplation of 'an action, or sentiment, or character'. The particular kind of pleasure or pain which constitutes the moral sense is partly specified by this specification of what induces it. Its being disinterested (like the aesthetic pleasure or pain with which Hume closely associates it) gives it further specification. Beyond that, Hume counts on our recognizing what he is referring to, when he calls this pleasurable or painful feeling a *moral* sense. But to press this point would be to enter unnecessarily upon a criticism of Hume's theory, when all we want to be able to do is to compare his notion of a moral sense with Newman's. In anticipation of this comparison, the thing especially to be noticed is that Hume's moral sense is not a cognitive sense; there is nothing it ascertains. Hume does speak, in passing, of the moral sense, as that 'by which moral good or evil is known', but the words are misleading; for, on the subjectivist view he is putting forward, to be morally good or evil is just to induce a particular kind of feeling: 'An action, or sentiment, or character is virtuous or vicious; why? because its view causes a pleasure or uneasiness of a particular kind.' There is nothing for the moral sense to ascertain, in a theory of this type. The features of an action—one of kindness, say— which induce a feeling of the appropriate kind, are ascertained by ordinary perception and whatever inference may be necessary, and not, of course, by the feeling induced. And that feeling and the features of the action are all that is relevant to the rightness or wrongness of the action, in this type of moral-sense theory.

The other type of moral-sense theory differs from this type in two respects. First, it is morally objectivist. It presupposes that the rightness or wrongness of an action, the goodness or badness of a person's character, exist independently of any feelings induced in us by the contemplation of an action or character of that sort. Ascertaining this rightness or wrongness

[3] *Treatise of Human Nature* (1739), bk. 3, pt. 1, § 2.

(goodness or badness), the moral sense it speaks of has a cognitive operation. The second point of difference between the two types of theory is that the proponents of the second type do not put forward a single description of the operation of the moral sense, no one description of its working which corresponds to the 'inducing', 'causing', 'exciting' of pleasure. The moral sense might be conceived of as analogous to sight; or (crossing the boundary between sense and intellect) as a seeing of self-evident truth. There might be no clear conception at all as to how it ascertains moral truth, as in Shaftesbury.

Shaftesbury (whose reduction of conscience to a mere moral sense we shall see criticized by Newman in the following chapter) was the most important proponent, historically, of the second type of moral-sense theory. Shaftesbury distinguishes, but most inconspicuously, between the cognitive and the affective in the operation of the moral sense. If the Shaftesburian descriptions of the moral sense were all a reader had to go on, he might possibly think he had imagined this duality in its operation, that its working was in fact purely affective, a unique kind of liking or aversion, an affection towards what is beautiful in disposition and conduct and an aversion from what is deformed. But then there would be no place in the picture for what Shaftesbury strongly asserted an 'immutable' and 'independent' right and wrong[4]—none at least for our knowledge of it. A point in Shaftesbury's conception of the moral sense is worth incidental notice. To say, speaking as any of us might, that a person lacks a moral sense is to criticize him for a moral defect; there is something seriously wrong with his character. In moral-sense theory, as a rule, the remark would not have this import. Shaftesbury is unusual amongst moral-sense theorists in the link he forges between moral sense and moral character. His moral sense is so closely allied to the social affections as at times to appear to merge into them. (For Newman also there is a necessary connection between a person's capacities in moral perception and his character, but not just with one feature of it—with his whole moral being.)

Common to the subjectivist and to the objectivist types of

---

[4] See Shaftesbury's *Inquiry Concerning Virtue or Merit* (bk. 1, pt. 2, § 3), one of the treatises in *Characteristics* (1711).

moral-sense theory, fundamental to the notion of a moral sense, is one feature of the way in which the moral sense is held to operate: it operates without ratiocination, with the immediacy of feeling. Reasoning will often be necessary to establish relevant matters of fact; for example, the circumstances of an action or its bearing on the happiness of those coming within range of it. But once these matters of fact are taken to be established, inference or the adducing of reasons is over. Some form of feeling or perceiving takes over, 'presenting' the action (the word is vague enough to straddle both types of moral-sense theory) as right or wrong.

The natural model for a moral sense which is to perceive a right or wrong which our feelings do nothing to constitute is provided by the external senses, for we take them to present us with what exists altogether independently of ourselves.[5] Throughout the life of moral-sense theory, however, there was a pervasive analogy between the moral sense and an 'inward sense', as it was sometimes called—the sense of beauty. The analogy is to be found in both Hume and Shaftesbury. Its tendency is to produce an account of the working of the moral sense appropriate to a subjectivist view of right and wrong, for the sense of beauty appears at least to lend itself readily to definition simply in terms of a disposition to receive pleasure or pain of a particular kind from the contemplation of an object. A moral sense analogous to the sense of beauty would be analogously defined. The analogy controls Newman's account of the determination of right and wrong by conscience as a moral sense, which we now consider, and explains its remarkably Humean appearance.

II

Encountered in isolation, the passage quoted at the beginning of the previous section of this chapter, in which Newman

[5] The external senses are taken as the model for an objectivist moral sense in an anticipatory version of moral-sense theory contained in Thomas Burnet's *Remarks upon an Essay Concerning Humane Understanding* (1697), and again by Thomas Reid when he countenanced moral-sense language (*Essays on the Active Powers of Man* (1788), ess. 5, ch. 8).

speaks of conscience as being 'a moral sense' and 'a sense of duty', 'a judgment of the reason' and 'a magisterial dictate', would not be read as requiring interpretation in accordance with the moral-sense tradition. It could be supposed that he was using the term 'moral sense' merely to designate conscience viewed as determining right and wrong in whatever way or ways it might do this; with no implication, therefore, that it does this in an operation characterized by the immediacy of feeling. It might even be supposed that the second of the coupled expressions—'a moral sense', 'a judgment of the reason'—was meant to explain the first; so that he is to be understood as maintaining that conscience effects its determination of right and wrong by reasoning. But though 'a judgment of the reason' could suggest 'dictamen rationis', and thus summon up the account of conscience given by Aquinas, according to which the judgement of conscience is the *conclusion* that this is to be done and that avoided,[6] the setting of the phrase here is incompatible with any ratiocinative implications it might otherwise carry, if it is understood as paraphrasing 'a moral sense'. It occurs after Newman has completed his description of what takes place in the determination of right and wrong by conscience as a moral sense. We are about to look at this. It will be seen that no activity of reason whatsoever is involved. In relation to the process Newman describes the phrase 'a judgment of the reason' is an extraneous formula. If it had been meant to designate anything in the process, the 'reason' it mentions would have been on this occasion, with Newman, the 'reason' which has often made its appearance on the pages of philosophers—one from which no reasoning comes.[7]

---

[6] *Summa Theologica*, 1a2ae, Q. 19, A. 5; 1a, Q. 79, A. 13. In § 5 of the Letter to the Duke of Norfolk (1875) Newman draws from Aquinas, half in quotation, half in paraphrase, a definition according to which conscience is 'the practical judgment or dictate of reason' regarding what is to be done as good or avoided as bad in concrete matters.

[7] Newman was greatly opposed to such a use of the word 'reason'. How the word should be used, how he himself used it, is a sizeable theme in the essay 'Revelation in its Relation to Faith'. He uses it, properly he believes, to signify 'the faculty of Reasoning in a large sense' (*Stray Essays*, p. 71). Later in the same essay Newman asserts the existence of a faculty which 'acts as a complement to reasoning', as being' the apprehension of first principles'. Even within this essay it is clear that not everything called by Newman a first principle is conceived by him as intuitively

Having mentioned other elementary constituents of our nature besides conscience—memory, reason, imagination, and 'the sense of the beautiful'—Newman explains how right and wrong are brought to our knowledge by conscience as a moral sense:

as there are objects which, when presented to the mind, cause it to feel grief, regret, joy, or desire, so there are things which excite in us approbation or blame, and which we in consequence call right and wrong; and which, experienced in ourselves, kindle in us that specific sense of pleasure and pain, which goes by the name of a good or bad conscience. (p. 105)

The ellipticality occurring when a good or bad conscience is mentioned is intensified in what is said a moment later to the point of producing the appearance of a different account of what takes place in consequence of which we call things right or wrong:

The feeling of conscience (being, I repeat, a certain keen sensibility, pleasant or painful,—self-approval and hope, or compunction and fear,—attendant on certain of our actions, which in consequence we call right or wrong) is twofold:—it is a moral sense, and a sense of duty . . . (p. 105)

Newman could now seem to be saying that following upon our doing certain things, we feel self-approval or its opposite, and that in consequence—*retrospectively*—we call things right or wrong: right, since doing them resulted in self-approval; wrong, since doing them resulted in self-condemnation. He is of course stating a single view, which is that the contemplation of certain things induces in us a feeling of approbation or disapprobation, in consequence of which we call these things right or wrong, and adding that the doing of these things evokes in us further correspondent pleasurable or painful feeling.

An immediate effect of this account of the determination of right and wrong by conscience as a moral sense is to occasion a doubt as to whether Newman's moral objectivism is too easily supposed. It is a doubt without substance. Newman's moral objectivism does not have to be inferred, though it can be securely inferred: an objectivist position has been avowed earlier in the *Grammar of Assent* (ch. 4, § 1, p. 65). Just possibly, Newman's account of the operation of conscience as a moral sense is itself much less Humean than it appears. The possibility is suggested by Newman's language at one point in a passage in the *Grammar of Assent*, in which the moral sense and the sense of beauty have briefly described parallel operations. (Obscuring an understanding of what Newman takes to occur when the moral sense and the sense of beauty come into operation is the fact that the description he provides is altogether incidental to his purpose, which is to contrast the 'notional assent' given to propositions such as 'There is a right and a wrong', 'a beautiful and a deformed', with the 'real assent' given to propositions which directly embody 'particular experiences of qualities in the concrete'.) This is the passage:

As we form our notion of whiteness from the actual sight of snow, milk, a lily, or a cloud, so, after experiencing the sentiment of approbation which arises in us on the sight of certain acts one by one, we go on to assign to that sentiment a cause, and to those acts a quality, and we give to this notional cause or quality the name of virtue, which is an abstraction, not a thing. And in like manner, when we have been affected by a certain specific admiring pleasure at the sight of this or that concrete object, we proceed by an arbitrary act of the mind to give a name to the hypothetical cause or quality in the abstract, which excites it. We speak of it as beautifulness, and henceforth, when we call a thing beautiful, we mean by the word nothing else than a certain quality of things, which creates in us this special sensation. (*Grammar of Assent*, ch. 4, § 1, pp. 64–5)

It might be that Newman is saying of the sentiment of approbation something that would be impossible on a Humean view, namely that it is 'caused'—not by the quality of an act (considerateness or whatever it might be) as a result of which the act is virtuous—but by the quality of virtue itself. Since it is an implication of the analogy between the sense of beauty and the moral sense that virtue and beauty have the same status, what is to be made of the 'quality of things', which creates in us aesthetic pleasure? On a Humean view, there is no shadow of doubt as to what this is. It is a 'structure of parts',[8] something literally seen or heard—not something present in what is seen or heard, a metaphysical quality, divined by a sense of beauty. Newman would have to be understood to be expressing the view Hume's view of beauty is contrasted with, if any weight is to be attached to the suggestion carried by his words that the sentiment of approbation is excited, not by what makes an act 'virtuous', right, but by its rightness.

Suppose that in the analogy he draws between the moral sense and the sense of beauty, Newman does think of beauty as being a metaphysical quality. Then his account of the operation of conscience as a moral sense contains latently an un-Humean complication. A sufficient indication of what it would be can be borrowed from Hume. 'We do not infer a character to be virtuous, because it pleases', Hume says; in Hume's view, its pleasing us in 'a particular manner' *is* its being virtuous (*Treatise of Human Nature,* bk. 3, pt. 1, § 2). On the interpretation of Newman's account of the moral-sense operation of conscience now being outlined, the rightness and wrongness of an action would be inferred from the way we feel about it. (This 'inference' would not be inconsistent with the unratiocinative character of a moral sense; no reasoning would be involved; the inference would be divinatory.) Suppose that Newman did not think of beauty as a metaphysical quality. Then he was led by the notion of an analogy between the moral sense and the sense of beauty into giving an account of the moral-sense operation of conscience appropriate, not to his own view, but to a subjectivist view of the distinction between right and wrong.

The most important question with regard to Newman's view of conscience which a reading of the *Grammar of Assent* could occasion, is whether he saw conscience as always effecting its determination of right and wrong in a moral-sense manner. A possible misunderstanding arising from what has been our most recent concern needs to be removed. Determination of right and wrong, by means of certain feelings elicited by an action, would be beside the point. That is a piece of moral-sense theorizing, easily shed. Presupposed by

[8] *Treatise of Human Nature*, bk. 2, pt. 1, § 8.

any moral-sense theorizing is what is fundamental to the notion of a moral sense, that it operates unratiocinatively, as the senses are naturally taken to do. The question would be whether it is Newman's view that conscience invariably proceeds in this manner in its determination of right and wrong. Except for the isolated phrase 'a judgment of the reason', everything that we have so far seen (and, as we shall see, the relevance of anything else in the *Grammar of Assent* has to be argued for) suggests that this is his view.

Whether Newman adds a ratiocinative operation to the moral-sense operation of conscience, whether his moral-sense language is to be taken at its face-value, whether the two primary sources for his view as to the way in which conscience ascertains right and wrong—the *Grammar of Assent* and the *University Sermons*—are mutually consistent, are matters which will occupy us for most of the rest of this chapter.

III

The *University Sermons,* preached before the University of Oxford between 1826 and 1843, anticipate the *Grammar of Assent* not only in their principal theme—they are 'chiefly on the theory of religious belief'—but also in a frequent general coincidence of position. Newman reissued the *Sermons* in 1871, the year after the *Grammar* was published.

A passage in the sermon 'The Usurpations of Reason' (1831) seems to ascribe astonishing capacities to conscience:

so alert is the instinctive power of an educated conscience, that by some secret faculty, and without any intelligible reasoning process, it seems to detect moral truth wherever it lies hid, and feels a conviction of its own accuracy which bystanders cannot account for; and this especially in the case of Revealed Religion, which is one comprehensive moral fact . . .[9]

Nothing like the claim for the theological competence of conscience, with which this passage seems to end, is made by

---

[9] *University Sermons* (3rd edn., 1871), 66. Individual sermons will usually be referred to by their number, not their title. The adding of a sermon, No. 3, in the 3rd edn. makes its numbering differ by one from that of the previous edns.

Newman when he undertakes to show elsewhere how we can come by way of our conscience to a realization that God exists. As we shall find, he there works with an everyday conception of conscience. Nor is the conscience brought by him into relation with ecclesiastical authority, endowed with extra-ordinary powers. There is development in Newman's conception of conscience, but not a great deal of it; and what development there is is not from any position expressed by the statements in this quotation, not, at least, until their language is heavily discounted. The development is in the direction of confining the deliverances of conscience to one's own actions and oneself.[10]

Something of what Newman was going to mean by an extension and magnification of the powers of conscience, which is incomprehensible when this quotation is lifted from its context, is disclosed when, just before it begins, he speaks of Christianity as bearing on its face 'the signs of a divine ordinance in the very same way in which the visible world attests to us its own divine origin', signs discernible to 'plain sense and religiously trained reason'. A further moderation of what is claimed for conscience comes when the passage ends with a saying of Christ's: 'I know My sheep, and am known of Mine.' Revealed Religion is not being made to stand before a self-assured conscience and be judged.

In later sermons Newman does a good deal to make intelligible the process by which conscience is able to detect hidden moral truth. A footnote comment, added in the third edition of the *University Sermons*, identifies the process as being 'an *implicit* act of reasoning'. With Newman these words, and the more usual 'implicit reasoning', do not stand for an empty notion, as in themselves they so easily might.

[10] How little Newman's view of the religious significance of conscience developed can be seen when the theology of conscience, as summarized in the sermon 'Natural and Revealed Religion Compared in Point of Influence' is viewed alongside the theology of conscience, as set out in the *Grammar of Assent*. This sermon was preached in 1830, a year and a half before the sermon just now quoted from. It is this earlier sermon which has the footnote reference to a passage in Coleridge—pointed out to Newman by a friend—which, Newman says, anticipates several points in his sermon (*University Sermons*, p. 23; the reference is to *Biographia Literaria* (1817), i. 196–9). The anticipation is almost all imaginary. As to conscience in particular, the passage in Coleridge merely states that 'the law of conscience peremptorily commands' belief in God as maker and judge.

Newman gives instances which incline one to acknowledge that what is pointed to is genuine reasoning, reasoning of which the reasoner is unaware, and in which the grounds of inference may be only adumbrated. We can often infer from, say, their religious or moral views, where certain persons will stand on matters which are apparently indifferent, and can often 'defend them far better than they defend themselves' (Sermon No. 11, p. 211). Implicit reasoning is contrasted with 'argument'. People 'may argue badly, but they reason well; that is, their professed grounds are no sufficient measures of their real ones'. They reach conviction not normally as a result of some proof seen as decisive, but as a result of many minute considerations coming together, which the mind cannot 'count up and methodize in argumentative form' (Sermon No. 13, p. 274). (This is one of the grounds for Newman's attack on writers, such as Paley, of the school of Christian evidences: they—and their confuters—deal only in the abstractions of argument.)

The relation between conscience and reason is only touched on in the *University Sermons*. It is the subject of a very opaque remark which is made before the notion of implicit reasoning has recognizably appeared. The setting of the remark is a contrast between faith and conscience taken together, and reason. By 'reason' Newman means, of course, reasoning. But, further, he means reasoning of the kind he will later call 'explicit'. This reasoning is articulated argument which results, Newman obscurely says, from an 'analysis' of what goes on in implicit reasoning. The presence of both these features of explicit reasoning will be noticed in the remark on the relation between conscience and reason. This is the remark:

No one will say that Conscience is against Reason, or that its dictates cannot be thrown into an argumentative form; yet who will, therefore, maintain that it is not an original principle, but must depend before it acts, upon some previous processes of Reason? Reason analyzes the grounds and motives of action: a reason is an analysis, but is not the motive itself. As, then, Conscience is a simple element in our nature, yet its operations admit of being surveyed and scrutinized by Reason; so may Faith be cognizable, and its acts be justified, by Reason, without therefore being, in matter of fact, dependent upon it . . . (*University Sermons*, No. 10, p. 193)

How would this passage be read by someone ignorant of Newman's notion of implicit reasoning (which, though unnamed, is unmistakably present in Sermon No. 11 preached a week later)? It would easily be read as having conscience determine right and wrong and as having it do this without reasoning, altogether non-inferentially—with what might be called logical immediacy. Even should it be supposed, at the prompting of the word 'motive', that a contrast is drawn between conscience as moving us to action in accordance with a conviction on right and wrong, and reason as motivationally inert, it could not be supposed that only as a principle of action is conscience 'an original principle'. Taken by itself, the passage readily and falsely suggests two sources of the knowledge of right and wrong, an unratiocinative conscience, and reason (with the judgements of conscience subject to correction by reason).

A contrast between perception by the senses and reasoning, made by Newman on several occasions, can be used to bring out the fundamental difference between the true and the false reading of the passage we are examining. In this contrast the senses give us 'direct and immediate acquaintance' with their objects, whereas knowledge obtained by reasoning is obtained 'indirectly', obtained 'upon grounds' (*University Sermons*, No. 11, pp. 205-7). The moral-sense perception, which the passage read in isolation can seem to be attributing to conscience, is analogous to sense perception in the respect in which Newman contrasts sense perception and reasoning (implicit as well as explicit reasoning). The moral sense has a 'direct and immediate' awareness of its object, the rightness or wrongness of an action, as the senses have of their objects; its operation, that is, is altogether non-inferential, is one of the logical immediacy. What moral-sense perception and the implicit reasoning, which is in fact assigned to conscience in the passage, have deceptively in common is *psychological* immediacy, an absence of any experience of mental process. A difficulty for the distinction between moral-sense perception and implicit moral reasoning needs to be obviated. It might be objected that Newman's contrast between sense perception and reasoning is too sharply drawn. Take a simple example of implicit reasoning (one Newman uses), the prediction of what the weather is going to be by someone who has learnt to read its antecedent signs. We learn to perceive (it might be said) in the same sort of way, finding out by experience the association of characteristics of perceivable things. The difficulty raised by this point can be bypassed. Moral-sense perception would have as its strict analogue, not the perception of complex objects, such as clouds and rain, but the perception by the senses of their 'proper' objects, to employ the old term. Colour, for example, is the proper object of sight. We do not have to learn to perceive colours, as we do to perceive complex objects. And just as without sight colour would be unknown, so without a moral perception working non-inferentially—its proponent contends—there would be no access to the elements of moral knowledge because, in his view, here there are no grounds for inference.

The evidence so far that moral reasoning is assigned to conscience in the *University Sermons* is the interpretation of a difficult passage in the very clear light of what is subsequently to be found in the *Sermons*, and Newman's note added in the third edition of the *Sermons*, that an obscurely described process of conscience is one of implicit reasoning. More evidence is available, though it is indirect.

That conscience engages in implicit reasoning is a corollary of the undeveloped comparison between conscience and faith. In the sermon containing the passage we examined just now, faith and reason are contrasted as though they were quite different (partly in ironic recognition of the fact that they are commonly thought to be so). Completing his account of their relationship, Newman maintains in the sermon following this one that a process of reasoning takes faith to the assent in which it terminates:

Consider the preternatural sagacity with which a great general knows what his friends and enemies are about and what will be the final result, and where, of their combined movements,—and then say whether, if he were required to argue the matter out in word or on paper, all his most brilliant conjectures might not be refuted, and all his producible reasons exposed as illogical.

And, in an analogous way, Faith is a process of the Reason, in which so much of the grounds of inference cannot be exhibited, so much lies in the character of the mind itself, in its general view of things . . . that it will ever seem to the world irrational . . . (*University Sermons*, No. 11, pp. 217–8)

If conscience is like faith, in what respect is there likeness between them? In this respect certainly: that the action of both involves their operating inferentially, but not by way of articulated inferences.

Several considerations make it an important question, whether Newman sees moral reasoning as an activity of conscience. One related to what we have been looking at over the last few pages is this: the notion that moral truth in complex cases could be ascertained as though by feeling or sight produces blank incomprehension; but let conscience be allowed implicit reasoning, and its power to detect hidden moral truth takes on intelligibility. And that it should be an 'educated' conscience to which Newman has attributed this power falls into place. Drawing upon experience is often a feature of implicit reasoning, as in the instance of the great general. When the right course of action is the one that will turn out best, the power of a conscience educated by experience to hit on this would be very understandable. More widely, experience would count in the assembling of relevant considerations and in the detection of their bearing upon one another, when right and wrong are determined by implicit reasoning.

It can be taken, then, to be the doctrine of the *University Sermons* that conscience engages in moral reasoning of an implicit kind. But it is part of the notion of implicit reasoning that no process of reasoning is experienced; no process of any kind.[11] Implicit reasoning is characterized by psychological immediacy. Determining the rightness or wrongness of an action by implicit reasoning, conscience would obtain its result as if this simply presented itself, as if the rightness or wrongness of the action was seen or felt.

[11] It 'shows as a simple act, not as a process, as if there were no medium interposed between antecedent and consequent, and the transition from one to the other were of the nature of an instinct,—that is, the process is altogether unconscious and implicit.' This description of implicit reasoning (under the name of 'natural inference') comes from the *Grammar of Assent* (ch. 8, § 3, p. 330).

The distinction between logical and psychological immediacy enables us to state a policy which has an application to several areas of Newman's thought. The attempt should always be made to take everything in Newman which is moral-sense or, more generally, intuitionist in appearance at less than its face value; partly because it can be seen, once the notion of implicit reasoning is understood, both that the appearance is likely to be misleading and how it could arise, and partly because a writer should be given the benefit of the doubt when there is a question as to whether or not he holds an epistemologically mysterious view. The distinction between logical and psychological immediacy needs to be kept constantly in mind. The moral sense or intuition of the theorist discerns this to be right and that wrong with logical immediacy, that is non-inferentially; no deductive step is taken, no reason adduced. It operates also with psychological immediacy; no mental process of any kind is experienced as gone through. The occurence of the second immediacy without the first can be illustrated by any of the uncontroversial intuitions we hear about, a wife's or a sailor's intuition, for example. The sailor who knows that a storm is coming, and does not know how he knows this, is in fact reasoning inductively, going by signs whose significance he has learnt by experience, but he has nothing to report introspectively. Newman's description of reasoning 'in its ordinary exercise' is full of the language of immediacy. It is full of terms to be found in the vocabulary of moral-sense or intuitionist theory—terms such as 'sense', 'intuition', 'perception', 'instinct', even 'divination'. Again and again he would be misunderstood if he were thought to be substituting logically immediate insight for reasoning.[12] *Psychological*

---

[12] Consider the following extreme example: 'Religious truth is reached, not by reasoning, but by an inward perception. Anyone can reason; only disciplined, educated, formed minds can perceive.' Newman said this in a letter (8 Mar. 1843) to a Miss H., who was having to decide whether to become a Roman Catholic or stay an Anglican (*Letters and Correspondence of John Henry Newman*, ed. Anne Mozley (London, 1891), ii. 409–10). He was in the same predicament himself at the time and, as the *Essay on the Development of Doctrine* (1845) and the *Apologia* (1864) show, behind his conversion two years later is abundant reasoning—argument—as well as a perception of the significance of various considerations. Newman's statement in this letter was dictated by a pastoral intention. His correspondent needed discipline of mind more than answers to arguments. 'Nothing . . . is more important to you than habits of self-command, as you say yourself. You are overflowing with feeling and impulse.' No account of Newman's thought could be more misleading than one in which he is represented as *substituting* perception for reasoning in matters of religion.

immediacy in Newman, so far from disposing us to find logical immediacy, should have the opposite effect.

We return from the *University Sermons* to the *Grammar of Assent.* The interpretative policy with which we have returned, of attempting to take anything in Newman that is moral-sense or intuitionist in appearance at less than its face value, is the policy of trying to construe the language of immediacy in every instance as asserting only psychological, not logical immediacy. It encounters, however, the most intractable material in the passage quoted from the *Grammar of Assent,* in which Newman speaks of our calling things right or wrong in consequence of the feeling of approbation or disapprobation they excite in us.

IV

A general possibility of reconciling the stubbornly moral-sense with the ratiocinative in Newman's moral philosophy is suggested when, in the paragraph following upon his account of conscience as a moral sense, he turns to the second of the two aspects he distinguished in conscience, with these words:

Here I have to speak of conscience in the latter point of view, not as supplying us, by means of its various acts, with the elements of morals, such as may be developed by the intellect into an ethical code, but simply as the dictate of an authoritative monitor . . . (*Grammar of Assent,* ch. 5, § 1, p. 106)

The possible reconciliation of the moral-sense with the radiocinative would be along these lines: the 'elements of morals' would be discerned in a moral-sense way; from these elements as data, the moral principles of an ethical code would be derived by certain processes of reasoning; these principles would be premisses for inference to the rightness or wrongness of actions. Not a very informative summary, but the relevant material is extremely exiguous. Further, it has an incidental character. And this is true, in greater or lesser degree, of all the material for an account of Newman's view of conscience. All of it is found in relation to something else being dealt with, which is his primary concern at the time; and, as a consequence, some parts of an unassembled theory of conscience, so to speak, are hardly more than adumbrated, some are described but not explicated, and there are some which fit badly. Conscience is dealt with at some length in the *Grammar of Assent* in order to show how God can become a reality to us; it is glanced at in the *University Sermons* in illustration of the nature of faith and when a point is being made in criticism of an evidentialist approach to Christianity. The moral-sense aspect of conscience is dealt with incidentally to a concern with conscience as a magisterial dictate (for this is what will bring home to us the reality of God); and one consequence of its not having Newman's mind fixed upon it is that nothing is said before the topic is left which might unify the moral-sense conscience of the *Grammar of Assent* with the conscience of the *University Sermons* which engages in reasoning. The material for the slight indication given above, as to how, in general, the moral-sense might be reconciled with the ratiocinative in Newman's moral philosophy, comes from three quite different contexts.

The inescapability of a moral-sense or intuitionist component in moral knowledge was a fairly prominent idea in the British philosophical tradition. The 'first principles of morals, into which all moral reasoning may be resolved', Thomas Reid maintained, 'are perceived intuitively, and in a manner more analogous to the perceptions of sense than to the conclusions of demonstrative reasoning'.[13] Newman's morally-sensed 'elements' of morals will not, however, be moral principles, but just the opposite: they will be the rightness or wrongness of individual actions in fully determinate circumstances, from which principles will be ratiocinatively derived. 'First principles', 'the propositions with which we start in reasoning on any given subject matter', he says in the *Grammar of Assent*, are 'conclusions or abstractions from particular experiences'; they are not 'elementary truths prior to reasoning' (ch. 4, § 1, pp. 60–6). The moral principle chosen as an illustration of this view is the last word in abstraction. It is that there is a right and a wrong. But there is no reason to think that more would have been said about the derivation of a more specific moral principle, for Newman's primary concern is not

[13] Thomas Reid, *Essays on the Intellectual Powers of Man* (1785), ess. 7, ch. 2.

with the derivation of principles, but with the nature of the assent given to first principles. It is sufficient for his purposes merely to mention the procedure by which moral principles are obtained: we 'abstract and generalize' from 'particular experiences'. 'I am not of course dreaming of denying the objective existence of the Moral Law,' Newman says—not as might have been thought probable, in reference to his having just previously made foundational to the knowledge of this objective law a 'sentiment of approbation'. The remark is made in reference to the concrete particularity of the experience from which the law in its generality has to be reasoned to. (The continuation of the remark, however, asserts something very different from a sentiment of approbation—an 'instinctive recognition of the immutable difference in the moral quality of acts . . . elicited in us by one instance of them.') The procedure of abstraction and generalization is applied, of course, not to any sentiment of ours, but to what has been discerned, the rightness or wrongness of a particular action in a particular set of circumstances.

How we are to ascertain 'what is right and wrong in a particular case' is a question brought up in a late section of the *Grammar of Assent* (ch. 9, § 2, pp. 353–6), in a context in which neither conscience nor a moral sense is mentioned; in which, further, there is no sign of anything characteristically moral-sense—a striking illustration of the point made a moment ago, that an account of Newman's view of conscience has to be put together from material prepared for other purposes. What was said earlier in the *Grammar of Assent* about the determination of right and wrong might as well not have existed, for all the effect it has on what is now said. Newman's primary concern in this section of the *Grammar of Assent* is to explain by comparison with a parallel faculty, 'the illative sense', which he variously describes, bringing different aspects of it into view, as 'right judgment in ratiocination', a 'power of judging and concluding', 'the controlling principle in inferences' which are informal in character. Calling it a *sense* is to make a use of the word 'parallel to our use of it' in 'good sense' and 'common sense', Newman remarks (*Grammar*, ch. 9, introduction, p. 345); parallel to our use of it in 'a sense of beauty', he surprisingly adds. The faculty with which the illative sense is compared is Aristotle's 'phronesis'—'practical wisdom', as it is commonly rendered; 'judgment', in Newman's rendering of it.

In Newman's account of phronesis, how we are to ascertain 'what is right and wrong in a particular case' is one of the questions which no ethical system can answer; for an answer to this we have to go to the 'living intellect, our own, or another's'. An ethical system may supply 'laws, general rules . . . examples . . . landmarks, limitations . . . dinstinctions', but all these have to be applied; it can tell us that virtue lies between extremes, but cannot determine for an individual where the mean lies for him. Phronesis, arising out of native endowment, 'formed and matured by practice and experience', regulates judgement in these matters. It does not manifest itself, Newman continues, in any 'comprehension of the mutual relations of duty towards duty, or any consistency in its teachings'. It is

a capacity sufficient for the occasion, deciding what ought to be done here and now, by this given person, under these given circumstances. It decides nothing hypothetical, it does not determine what a man should do ten years hence, or what another should do at this time. It may indeed happen to decide ten years hence as it does now, and to decide a second case now as it now decides a first; still its present act is for the present, not for the distant or the future. (p. 355)

From phronesis 'the science of morals forms its rules'.

Our general interest in this account of phronesis is in its bearing on the possibility of a reconciliation between the moral-sense or intuitionist and the ratiocinative in Newman's view of moral knowledge. Our specific interest is in whether there can be obtained from it an indirect confirmation of the evidence provided by the *University Sermons*, that Newman attributed to conscience the power to reason. We first need to know how his conceptions of conscience and of phronesis are related.

Conscience and phronesis, as Newman describes it, are not one and the same thing. To treat them as if they were, as is sometimes done, is to bring inconsistency into Newman's mature conception of conscience at an important point. Conscience, which earlier in the *Grammar of Assent* has to do with 'self alone and one's own actions' (ch. 5, § 1, p. 107), would, if identical with phronesis, be pronouncing for another as well as for oneself. When Newman mentions resort to the 'living intellect' in his account of phronesis, it is resort, expressly, to our own intellect—'or another's'.

There is necessarily, however, a partial coincidence between conscience and phronesis in Newman's conception of them both. Phronesis decides 'what ought to be done here and now, by this given person, under these given circumstances'. So does conscience, in Newman's conception of it, provided that the person is oneself and the conduct one's own. There cannot be two distinct faculties, operating in the same way, the only difference between them being that the business of one of them is one's own conduct in particular circumstances and the business of the other someone else's conduct. And so when Newman mentions one's own conduct in the course of his account of phronesis, he is speaking appropriately when he says that it is in virtue of phronesis that the individual is 'his own law, his own teacher, and his own judge in those special cases of duty which are personal to him' (p. 354). Elsewhere —outside this specialized context—he would have said that each individual is his own law, teacher, and judge in these circumstances, in virtue of his conscience.

Given that under circumstances which are irrelevant to its nature as a faculty phronesis coincides with conscience, and that (like the illative sense it is explaining) its working involves inference, it follows that the working of conscience involves inference. This gives us a result in accordance with the ascription of implicit reasoning to conscience in the *University Sermons*. But what has become of the moral-sense operation which conscience had earlier in the *Grammar of Assent*?

There seems to be an obvious place for this in Newman's account of phronesis, provided the assumption is not made that, from start to finish, phronesis is to be regarded as strictly analogous to the illative sense, for on that assumption it will have no operation external to reasoning. A determination of right and wrong in a moral-sense manner seems to have a place left for it with the remark that 'the science of morals forms its rules' from phronesis. This remark appears to correspond to the remark earlier in the *Grammar of Assent* (ch. 5, § 1,

p. 106) that conscience supplies us 'with the elements of morals, such as may be developed by the intellect into an ethical code'. The context of the earlier remark requires it to be supposed that we are supplied with the elements of morals by conscience working as a moral sense. Accordingly, for there to be a real correspondence between the two remarks, it would have to be supposed that Newman attributed to phronesis a power of logically immediate moral perception. That supposed, the earlier and the later accounts of moral knowledge in the *Grammar of Assent* fit together and are complementary. In both there is an interest in moral particularity: in the earlier one, in moral particularity as a starting-point for the formation of moral rules; in the later one, in moral particularity as that which has to be reached, starting from moral rules. The formation of these rules, though not a matter of interest in the later account is referred to; and with regard to their formation, it is natural to suppose that phronesis does what the moral sense did in the earlier account.

The difficulty of supposing that in the *Grammar of Assent* a perceptual power of the appropriate kind is attributed to phronesis arises out of Aristotle's conception of this faculty, which in everything we have looked at Newman has made his own. As Aristotle conceived of it, phronesis, practical wisdom, has as its object human good and the way to attain it. Involved in practical wisdom are mastery of the principles of conduct, deliberative power, and—because this wisdom is practical—a perceptual power; for 'practice is concerned with particulars', 'since the thing to be done is of this nature', and particulars have to be perceived.[14] The question is as to the nature of these particulars, and so as to the nature of the perception by which they are apprehended. The right interpretation of Aristotle is not our concern—only Newman's understanding of him.

Phronesis, Newman says following Aristotle, is 'matured by practice and experience'. Now there certainly are exercises of moral judgement which can be improved by experience. No one, for example, is simply born with the capacity of telling how an action, harmless in appearance, is likely to turn out. Such perceptual judgements—distillations of experience—are

---

[14] *Nicomachean Ethics*, 1141^b–1142^a (W. D. Ross's translation).

of the very kind to be expected from phronesis. But a power of *logically immediate* moral perception is another matter altogether. How would improvement in its exercise be possible? By what standard would improvement be judged? These questions are not unanswerable. A moral sense or its intellectualist equivalent in a perceptual power of the kind under discussion, subject to correction by reason, could improve in performance, profiting by its mistakes. But the moral sense of the philosophical tradition to which the moral sense of the *Grammar of Assent* plainly belongs, apprehends that to which reason has no access because grounds for inference are taken to be absent. And by having the moral sense ascertain the elements of morals, Newman himself seems to imply that it perceives what cannot be inferred, giving moral reasoning a starting-point. A corresponding power of moral perception, incapable either of self-correction in its exercise or of external correction, would be anomalously attributed to phronesis.

There is a reason which is more directly related to Newman's understanding of Aristotle's text against supposing that phronesis in the *Grammar of Assent* has a power of logically immediate perception. A note of expository comment, written by Newman in his copy of Wilkinson's edition of the *Nicomachean Ethics*,[15] concerns itself in part with what is to be made of the perception spoken of by Aristotle (1142^a) as an activity of phronesis. This perception is said in the note to be 'tact from long experience approaching to a natural sense'. These words do not describe a power of logically immediate perception.

The moral sense is associated not with phronesis, but with another Aristotelian faculty, in the late essay of Newman's, referred to previously in this chapter in a different connection. Having objected to the use of the word 'reason' to designate mental proceedings which do not involve reasoning, Newman goes on to speak of 'a faculty in the mind which acts as a complement to reasoning', upon which reasoning is 'dependent',

---

[15] *Aristotelis Ethicorum Nicomacheorum libri decem*, ed. G. Wilkinson (4th edn., 1818), was the book used by Newman in teaching Aristotle's ethics at Oriel. (Newman was fellow of Oriel from 1822 to 1845.) The note is opposite pp. 247–8 of Wilkinson. Newman's copy of the book is in the archives at the Birmingham Oratory.

which has 'truth for its direct object'. Viewed 'in its relation to religion' (religion, not morality being the concern of the essay), this faculty is 'the moral sense'. In its wider scope as 'being the apprehension of first principles', it is, he says, the faculty called by Aristotle *noûs*.[16]

However casually on occasion Newman might use the term 'moral sense', he also has a strict conception of it. And these remarks make unmistakable two points in this conception. They are that as having moral truth for its direct object, moral-sense perception is to be contrasted with reasoning of any kind—with implicit reasoning no less than with explicit; and that moral reasoning is ultimately dependent upon moral-sense perception, or upon the intuition of its intellectualist equivalent.

V

What are we to conclude with regard to the way in which conscience effects the determination of right and wrong Newman assigns to it? We are to conclude that it sometimes simply perceives that an action is right or wrong, and sometimes infers this. The principal difficulties faced by this conclusion are that in the *University Sermons* the only operation conscience has is ratiocinative, and that in the *Grammar of Assent* there is no sign of the moral-sense operation, which conscience has early in the book, when later the determination of right and wrong in particular circumstances is again under consideration—no sign of it, and severe obstacles to finding a conjectural place for it. The difficulties greatly diminish when notice is taken of Newman's preoccupations in the writing that occasions them. Preoccupied with other matters in the various contexts in which he says things with a bearing on the determination of right and wrong by conscience, never having occasion to bring these things into one view, Newman says nothing that would enable us to see

---

[16] *Stray Essays*, pp. 97–8; cf. *Nicomachean Ethics* 1141^{a}5–8. Newman's notion of the moral sense (in an extended meaning of the term) as an instrument of religious discernment will be considered in the following chapter.

how the two different powers he attributes to conscience work together in everyday consciences.

It needs to be emphasized that Newman assigns to conscience both a moral-sense and a ratiocinative operation. That Newman assigns to conscience an operation that is strictly moral-sense, as being altogether non-inferential, needs emphasis because there seems to be a reluctance in commentators to recognize this, as there is to recognize that he sometimes uses the word 'instinctive' to designate one that is non-inferential in character. There is some indication of reluctance in Newman himself to recognize the moral-sense and intuitionist element in his thought. The following passage in one of his letters confirms the presence of this element:

You will find I there consider that the dictate of conscience is particular . . . and that from the multiplication of particulars I *infer* the general.

Next that this dictate of conscience . . . is a moral *instinct* and its own evidence—as the *belief* in an external world is an *instinct* on the apprehension of sensible phenomena.[17]

This 'instinct' is more than that of ordinary speech; its operation is characterized by more than psychological immediacy. Indicated by the words 'its own evidence' and by the comparison with 'instinctive' belief in an external world, it is an operation characterized also by logical immediacy.[18]

[17] Newman to Charles Meynell, 25 July 1869. Diffident about his knowledge of philosophy and of Catholic philosophy in particular, and anxious to keep within the bounds of 'doctrinal propriety', Newman had Meynell, who taught philosophy at the seminary at Oscott, go through the *Grammar of Assent* at proof stage. The Newman–Meynell correspondence is published as an appendix to Zeno's book, *John Henry Newman: Our Way to Certitude* (Leiden, 1957). It is also to be found in vol. xxiv of the *Letters and Diaries of John Henry Newman*, ed. Charles Stephen Dessain *et al.* (London and Oxford, 1961–).

[18] Meynell disliked the notion of a cognitive 'instinct' operating non-inferentially. A postscript in his letter of 27 Nov. 1869 to Newman contains the following remark: 'From one sentence [in the draft of the *Grammar of Assent*], where you essentially require media for ratiocination, I should infer that, if the process of instinctive inference could be recovered in consciousness, it would fall under the ordinary dialectic rules. If so, I want no theory for this kind of inference, and it is only stupidity which has prevented my seeing this. But I am not sure that I understand.' In both of the passages to which Meynell might be referring, reasoning is certainly being spoken of. In one (*Grammar*, ch. 8, § 3, pp. 330–1) it is said of the reasoning which is described that to 'the mind itself, the reasoning is a simple divination'; in the other (ch. 8, § 1, pp. 259–60), that we proceed 'by a sort of instinctive perception, from premiss to conclusion'. The passages illustrate Newman's notion of instinctive

That Newman assigns to conscience a ratiocinative operation needs to be emphasized on a number of grounds. First, we bring a contrary expectation to the reading of him: we never hear it said in ordinary, untheoretical talk about conscience that conscience draws inferences, arrives at conclusions, or does anything of the sort. Then, in the *Grammar of Assent*, in Newman's most systematic account of the nature and operations of conscience, the operation assigned to conscience in determining right and wrong is wholly moral-sense, altogether unratiocinative.

A further consideration is of a different kind. It bears on the reliability of conscience, which, in Newman's teaching, is to be our guide in all the various circumstances in which we find ourselves; to be our guide by determining for each of us the right thing to do in these circumstances. This will sometimes be obvious or easily discerned. When it is so, a conscience operating in a moral-sense manner would guide us safely. But there would be considerable risk in our being entrusted to a conscience which made such short work of difficult cases. It is important, then, that if conscience is to be assigned the office of determining what to command and prohibit, it be adequately equipped for the task. Whether or not Newman clearly envisaged the handling by conscience of cases of moral complexity, he made provision for it by making implicit reasoning an activity of conscience.

A question of particular importance arising earlier in the chapter has in effect been answered. The question was whether Newman is to be understood as holding conscience to a moral-sense type of operation whenever it engages in the determination of right and wrong, or as leaving quite open the way or ways in which it might operate—with reasoning therefore possibly among its resources. Putting the answer together: if reasoning is called for, conscience can reason. But a moral-sense characterization of its activity would not altogether fall away, for its reasoning would be of the kind Newman called implicit. And in reasoning of this kind, as he described it, the concluding is as if it was a perceiving.

apprehension when, clearly, only psychological immediacy is involved. They are no guide to his meaning when he speaks of conscience as a 'moral instinct and its own evidence', and of our believing on 'instinct' in an external world. Newman does not advert to Meynell's remark in the subsequent letter to him.

A 'moral sense' and a 'magisterial dictate': Newman's treatment of the magisterial aspect of conscience is the main subject of the next chapter, and in connection with this we shall have to look at the moral sense again. We shall not be bringing up for further elaboration any part of the discussion of conscience as a determiner of right and wrong in a moral-sense manner. Our interest will be in what Newman says about a falsifying of the nature of conscience produced by its reduction to a mere moral sense—not to the cognitive moral sense dealt with in this chapter, but to a moral sense with an aspect to it which might, with some show of plausibility, replace the magisterial aspect of conscience. We have one more thing to consider in this chapter: Newman's opinion that the act of conscience has, indivisibly, a cognitive aspect and a magisterial aspect. 'Of course its act is indivisible; still it has these two aspects, distinct from each other, and admitting of a separate consideration' (*Grammar of Assent*, ch. 5, § 1, pp. 105–6).

There is first a point to be made about the cognitive aspect of the act of conscience. This will be either an exercise of moral-sense perception, or a judgement of the reason. The two expressions, 'a moral sense', 'a judgment of the reason' are coupled immediately before Newman's remark comes. They are not synonymous; as we saw, the second one has no application to the moral-sense exercise of conscience which had just been described. We can take 'a judgment of the reason' to signify, as possibly Newman intended—though there is no mention in the *Grammar of Assent* of conscience as reasoning—the summing-up or concluding in which a process of the implicit reasoning, ascribed to conscience in the *University Sermons*, would terminate.

A comment is called for which would hold good whatever Newman might have had in mind by the indivisibility of the act of conscience. Normally, no deciding on right and wrong takes place before or as the imperative of conscience is felt, because normally none is needed. Brought up to know that lying is wrong, a person tempted to tell a downright lie does not have to ascertain anything in order to be in trouble with his conscience. The magisterial operation of conscience is not, then, one aspect of an indivisible act: its normal antecedent is a long-standing belief.[19]

When we look further, we see that the magisterial operation of conscience does not necessarily have as an antecedent a *moral* conviction at all; the belief that some injunction has divine authority would do instead.[20] Consider a clash of conscience over whether a child is to be given a blood transfusion in order to save its life. Governing the conscience of one person in the dispute is the taken-for-granted duty to do what can be done to save a human life. Governing the conscience of the other is something altogether different, the belief that God has prohibited blood transfusions, in the book of Leviticus. Argued with, he might possibly say that it would be morally wrong not to obey God and that none of God's injunctions could be morally wrong. These are background considerations if present at all, and, more important, they are general considerations. What specifically governs his conscience is the belief that blood transfusions are prohibited in the Word of God, a belief to which his conscience, of course, contributes nothing.

When conscience makes itself felt magisterially, there has to be something corresponding to what Newman saw as the cognitive side of its act. There has to be the belief (or suspicion, but we can neglect this complication here) that an action is morally right or wrong, or that it is required or forbidden in one's religion. This belief cannot always be ascribed to conscience: so much is clear from the case we have just now looked at. And as we saw a moment ago, there does not have to be, normally there is not, any determining of right

[19] Influenced by an entirely different consideration, Maurice Nédoncelle represents Newman as maintaining, not that the act of conscience is indivisible, but that it is 'often undivided' (*La Philosophie religieuse de J. H. Newman* (Strasburg, 1946), 91). Nédoncelle is influenced by Newman's saying at once that the act of conscience is indivisible and that its aspects are capable of separate consideration; as if in explanation, Newman goes on to speak, in a difficult passage, of the possibility of a sense of the moral deformity of an action without a sense of the obligation to abstain from it. The passage will be discussed in ch. 3.

[20] Why are the imperatives of conscience confined to matters of morality and religion? A reason would be that the imperatives of conscience are absolute—no accommodation can be struck with them—and only moral and religious considerations override, correspondingly, all other considerations. (Discussion of the matter would be out of place, but a believer in God necessarily sees religious and moral considerations as themselves harmonious.)

and wrong at all. Normally involved are only one's habitual moral or religious convictions, however these have been arrived at, and, instead of behaviour spontaneously in accordance with them, some disinclination to behave accordingly.

3

'A MAGISTERIAL DICTATE'

This is its primary and most authoritative aspect; it is the ordinary sense of the word. Half the world would be puzzled to know what was meant by the moral sense; but every one knows what is meant by a good or bad conscience. Conscience is ever forcing on us by threats and by promises that we must follow the right and avoid the wrong; so far it is one and the same in the mind of every one, whatever be its particular errors in particular minds as to the acts which it orders to be done or to be avoided . . . conscience . . . is concerned with persons primarily, and with actions mainly as viewed in their doers, or rather with self alone and one's own actions . . . (*Grammar of Assent*, ch. 5, § 1, pp. 106–7)

HAVING given an account of conscience as a moral sense, Newman has begun in this passage his treatment of conscience as a magisterial 'dictate' (or of its magisterial 'office'). A remark in the passage calls for an incidental comment. A good or bad conscience is unlikely to come quickly to mind, when we think of conscience as operating imperatively, as ordering this to be done, that to be avoided. We have a bad conscience over something done or, at any rate, resolved upon, not when we are experiencing the dictates of conscience. Newman was not, of course, ignorant of the conditions under which we have a bad conscience in the 'ordinary sense of the word', but his mind was on the sanction attached by conscience to its commands and prohibitions; and this sanction is at least in part the threat or anticipatory experience of a bad conscience. It is surprising, all the same, that the role around which most of the imagery of conscience clusters, its accusatory or condemnatory role, should be subordinated in this way to its imperatival role.

'A magisterial dictate', 'a sense of duty and obligation', 'a sanction of right conduct', are brief descriptions Newman gives of the aspect of conscience with which he is now concerned. There are differences between them. To the description of conscience as a magisterial dictate the other two make a contribution. The magisterial dictate of conscience is an imperative, commanding or prohibiting the doing of the things seen as right or wrong; a unique imperative, partly made so by the uniqueness of the sanction attached to it; a sense of the duty to do or abstain from the things seen as right or wrong, a sense—as Newman's use of the word 'obligation' conveys more strongly—of this doing or abstention as imposed upon us.

In its magisterial office conscience has a universality which it does not have in the conjoint office Newman assigned to it, that of determining right and wrong in the actual situations in which we find ourselves. Its imperatival dictates are 'one and the same in the mind of every one'; its determinations of right and wrong are subject to individual variation. (To everyone, however, it gives 'testimony that there is a right and a wrong', Newman says, though he would have to agree that this testimony is not among the deliverances of conscience but is extracted from them.) Our conscience commands the doing of what *we* see as right and prohibits our doing what we see as wrong. And in all of us alike its judgement falls on us for the thing *we* saw, or avoided seeing, as wrong and did; and for the thing we left undone, seeing it (or not letting ourselves see it) as required of us. The emphasis must not be misunderstood. Conscience, as there will be occasion to notice later, does not stamp approval on individual autonomy, most certainly not in Newman's account of it. It does not prompt us to attach any significance to a moral opinion as being our own. Its dictate requires us to do the thing we see as *right*.

I

The similarities and dissimilarities between conscience and aesthetic taste are regarded by Newman as very significant for an understanding of conscience. As we have 'a sense of duty and obligation', however different the actions engaging it, so we have 'a sense of the beautiful and graceful', for all its diversity in different persons (*Grammar of Assent*, ch. 5, § 1, p. 107). Both taste and conscience we have 'naturally'. (The question as to what Newman meant by this naturality is postponed until it can be given the space it needs.) But taste is self-contained, as conscience is not.

Conscience vaguely reaches forward to something beyond self, and dimly discerns a sanction higher than self for its decisions, as is evidenced in that keen sense of obligation and responsibility which informs them. And hence it is that we are accustomed to speak of conscience as a voice . . . and moreover a voice, or the echo of a voice, imperative and constraining, like no other dictate in the whole of our experience. (*Grammar of Assent*, ch. 5, § 1, p. 107)

This difference between conscience and aesthetic taste goes along with another stressed by Newman. Aesthetic taste has no essential connection with 'emotion'. Beauty is contemplated with tranquil admiration except when it is personal beauty; then emotion enters into the experience—affection or passion.

Conscience too, considered as a moral sense, an intellectual sentiment, is a sense of admiration and disgust, of approbation and blame: but it is something more than a moral sense; it is always, what the sense of the beautiful is only in certain cases; it is always emotional . . . it always implies what that sense only sometimes implies . . . it always involves the recognition of a living object, towards which it is directed. Inanimate things cannot stir our affections; these are correlative with persons. (p. 109)

As we shall see later in the chapter, Newman has in mind the theological implications of the phenomena of conscience in this mention of their emotional character and in making emotion 'correlative with persons'.

There is a philosophically induced diminution of conscience, Newman thought, in which it is turned into a mere moral sense by the transformation of its magisterial side into the affective side of the moral sense. With the transformation conscience becomes theologically silent. Its transformation in this manner is a theme in the eighth discourse of *The Idea of a University* (1852). Shaftesbury, in particular, is under criticism. To conscience reduced to a moral sense vice is a deformity (and therefore odious); virtue a species of beauty.

A bad conscience is 'not much more than the sort of feeling which makes us shrink from an instrument out of tune' (p. 197). In the view Newman is criticizing a bad conscience is, of course, more than that—his remark is made in comment upon a Shaftesburian rhapsody on the beauty of virtue in which a notion of the virtuoso makes its appearance. But a bad conscience, when conscience is only a moral sense, is only a feeling of degradation and shame. Missing from it are fear and foreboding.

Newman sees a morality that is purely moral-sense in character as one without the sense of obligation and prohibition, as this enters into our moral experience with the operation of conscience. Moral approbation and revulsion, even though grounded on what befits or affronts our nature, he sees as simply discontinuous with our experience of that obligation and that prohibition:

Though I lost my sense of the obligation which I lie under to abstain from acts of dishonesty, I should not in consequence lose my sense that such actions were an outrage offered to my moral nature. Again; though I lost my sense of their moral deformity, I should not therefore lose my sense that they were forbidden to me. (*Grammar of Assent*, ch. 5, § 1, p. 106)

This is a difficult passage. It can seem to contradict the remark which it immediately follows; according to which the act of conscience has, indivisibly, two aspects, one determinative of what is to be done, the other magisterially requiring that it be done. Is it now being said that we might see something as wrong and yet have no sense of an obligation to abstain from it? A supposable absence of a sense of obligation to abstain from conduct seen as dishonest: how is that compatible with the indivisible unity of the act of conscience?

Take Newman to be contrasting a morality with a moral sense but without conscience, and a morality with conscience but no moral sense, and there is no longer a problem about the relationship between what he is now saying and what he has just said. In the morality without conscience the moral deformity of an action will be perceived, but there will be no sense of obligation (at least none of the kind brought by conscience) to abstain from it. In the morality without a moral

sense there will be a sense of forbiddenness, but it will not be
occasioned by a perception of moral obliquity. What, then,
would elicit it? Since conscience is engaged, and not over
moral right and wrong, presumably there would be involved
belief in the divine prohibition of an action—like the
prohibition in the Garden of Eden. These moralities are only
what might have been. We have both a moral sense and a
conscience; or, Newman chooses to say, the moral-sense and
the magisterial are aspects of the unitary act of conscience.

The moral sense in the passage before us is given a
Shaftesburian description; and to the extent to which the
moral sense, as Shaftesbury conceived of it, is merely
aesthetic—its object 'the *venustum* . . . the *decorum* of
things'[1]—the notion of obligation is alien to it. For Newman
too the moral sense is not only analogous to a sense of beauty
and ugliness, but as he indicated in the course of his
comparison between conscience and aesthetic taste, it can be a
sense of moral beauty and ugliness. An idea made familiar by
Paley also helps to make more readily understandable Newman's
asserting the separability of a sense of obligation from the
moral sense. In total contrast with anything moral-sense in
nature, Paley had made very familiar the idea that obligation
has an external character. The various answers to the
question, Why are we obliged to keep our word?—'Because it
is right' . . . 'Because it promotes the public good'—Paley
maintained, 'all leave the matter *short*'. To complete the
answer he added two considerations different in kind from
such considerations as these. The first of them was that
entering into the idea of obligation 'is the idea of command,
authority, law, or the will of a superior'; for something to be
obligatory, regardless of its own nature, the doing of it must
be imposed.[2] Up to a point, Paley might almost be characterizing the magisterial aspect of the dictate of conscience as
Newman describes it. (In Paley himself conscience is a slight
thing.) Even the second consideration added by Paley
corresponds up to a point with a feature of the magisterial
operation of conscience as described by Newman—its 'forcing

[1] Shaftesbury, *Sensus Communis*, pt. 4, § 2, in *Characteristics*. This quotation is
among those from Shaftesbury in the 8th discourse of *The Idea of a University*.
[2] William Paley, *Moral and Political Philosophy* (1785), bk. 2, chs. 1, 2.

on us by threats and by promises that we must follow the right and avoid the wrong'. 'As we should not be obliged to obey the laws,' Paley said, 'unless rewards or punishments . . . depended upon our obedience; so neither should we, without the same reason, be obliged to do what is right' (bk. 2, ch. 2).

It needs to be emphasized that it is the *sense* of obligation which Newman asserts to be separable from perception by the moral sense. (He is not asserting an opinion at odds with such facts as that to describe a thing as bad, let alone as wrong, is to prescribe its avoidance.) And beyond his intentions, his phenomenology of conscience—which is no set piece, but is conveyed in a few paragraphs and phrases—makes apparent the *experiential* discontinuity between the operation of conscience given a moral-sense aspect, and its magisterial dictate. His concern with the phenomena of conscience, as we are about to see, is in order to explain how a consciousness of God as Ruler and Judge is possible; and so it is a concern with a magisterial conscience and with a bad and a good conscience. It was no part of Newman's purpose to show what corresponds experientially to conscience thought of as determining right and wrong. Not much reflection is needed, however, to make it apparent that had it been so, there is nothing to which he could have pointed. There are no phenomena associated with the determination of right and wrong. We might report that the right thing to do just came to us, or we might mention various considerations which led us to a conclusion, or one that counted decisively with us. Since the characteristic phenomena of conscience are so strongly associated with the idea of conscience, their absence when an honest effort is being made to determine right and wrong points to the arbitrariness of ascribing to conscience any determination of right and wrong.

The difference between conscience as a moral sense and conscience as a magisterial dictate is so great in kind for Newman that he calls the one 'the principle of ethics', the other 'the creative principle of religion' (*Grammar of Assent*, ch. 5, § 1, p. 110). What he had in mind in calling conscience as a moral sense the principle of ethics is pretty conjectural. The moral sense as a sense of moral beauty and deformity, or of what is due to our nature, would be involved, if at all, in an altogether subordinate way. Newman's reference to the moral sense as the principle of ethics has some explanation in the equally brief remark made several pages earlier (p. 106), that conscience as a moral sense supplies us 'by means of its various acts, with the elements of morals'. If the elucidation of this remark in the previous chapter is on the right lines, his main idea in regarding the moral-sense operation of conscience as the principle of ethics would be that foundational to ethics is a moral-sense or intuitive apprehension of the rightness or wrongness of actions in their full particularity.

In an extension of the meaning of the term, the moral sense is sometimes with Newman a power of perception in matters of religion. The acuity of the moral sense proper has a dependence upon our moral character, Newman held. Correspondingly, for this power of religious perception to exist, it is necessary that the 'heart' be right. This is the power referred to in one of the *Late Essays* when (as we saw in the previous chapter) a faculty of first principles is mentioned complementary to the faculty of reason. The reference to it in that context creates the impression that it is thought of as the source of the most elementary truths of religion from which reasoning might then proceed. The same impression is given in a note to the sermon 'The Usurpations of Reason' in the third edition of the *University Sermons*, when it is said that 'the moral sense must supply us with the assumptions to be used as premisses in religious inquiry' (p. 55). The note is awkwardly related to the text and obscures its meaning, which has to do with the attitude brought to reasoning in matters of religion and its effect on what is made of the considerations that come up, 'spiritual discernment' being the judge. As used by Newman in connection with religion, the term 'moral sense' much more nearly designates the right attitude, if truth is to be obtained, than a source of premisses. There are no intuitively ascertained premisses in his theology which enable reasoning to get under way. The evidences of design in Nature have been thought of by many as a starting-point for theistic reasoning. In Newman's view they commend themselves to a mind already religious. It is not conscience as a 'moral sense', in any meaning of the term, but conscience as a 'magisterial dictate', which is foundational to religion.

II

Conscience as a 'magisterial dictate'—the term having to be understood in this connection as covering the accusatory or condemnatory operation of conscience as well as its imperatival operation, since a bad conscience is of such significance—is 'the creative principle of religion' because its phenomena 'avail to impress the imagination with the picture of a Supreme Governor, a Judge, holy, just, powerful, all-seeing, retributive' (*Grammar of Assent*, ch. 5, § 1, p. 110). Its phenomena are states of mind with implicit reference to a personal being. They are, in Newman's phenomenology of conscience, mostly dark, at least the intense ones are: fear and foreboding (' "The wicked flees, when no one pursueth;" then why does he flee?'), shame (when there are no witnesses).[3] There is, however, contrition as well as remorse. And 'when the conscience is good', there are the contraries of the dark states of mind. Newman mentions peace, a sense of security, lightness of heart, hope.

One question about Newman's 'proof of theism' can be conveniently raised now while we have before us a specification of the phenomena from which it proceeds. Let it be allowed that the phenomena of a conscience commanding and prohibiting, and accusing or condemning, point to the existence of a God who is holy, all-seeing, retributive. What in our experience of the working of conscience points in a similar way to loving-kindness and mercy in God? Lightness of heart and hope? But are they ever induced by the working of conscience? If it is objected that the question is tendentiously expressed because the phrase 'the working of conscience' is associated with the thought or urgent, disturbing, or painful feeling, it can be asked instead, avoiding any idiomatic expression, whether lightness of heart or hope is ever due to conscience. A good conscience, coupled with the thought of a judgement to come, might induce such states of mind. But as far as one can see, a setting of religious belief or half-belief needs to be

---

[3] In one place Newman links the origin of conscience with the Fall: 'They lost Eden, and they gained a conscience' (*Parochial and Plain Sermons*, viii. 258, No. 18). In a later work, and looking at conscience from a different point of view, he links the origin of conscience, as we shall see, with Creation.

presupposed for a good conscience to have this effect; by itself it generates nothing whatever of religious import. Hope and lightness of heart are states of mind too positive to be attendant upon the mere possession of a good conscience; all that seems to bring is an untroubled mind. The mark of a good conscience is an absence of the phenomena of conscience.

Newman regarded the transition of the mind from the phenomena of conscience to an awareness of God as being analogous to what he thought took place in other connections. As from 'a multitude of instinctive perceptions . . . of something beyond the senses, we generalize the notion of an external world . . . so from the perceptive power which identifies the intimations of conscience with the reverberations . . . of an external admonition, we proceed to the notion of a supreme Ruler and Judge' (*Grammar of Assent*, ch. 5, § 1, p. 104). He has another analogy also strongly in mind. This analogy is with the way children, and even animals (the dog knows its owner as the infant does its mother), discern 'amid the maze of colours and shapes which meet their sight', 'unseen' beings, unseen as the unitary beings they are. The obscurity of what Newman has in mind here as known need not trouble us—'certain units, individuals, substances, whatever they are to be called, which are outside and out of the reach of sense' (p. 103). Our interest is in what is for him a way of knowing. All we need initially to be sure of, as we can be, is that here he sees as known something quite other than a mere conjunction of phenomena with phenomena. Phenomena, 'impressions', can disclose what transcends them. Newman emphasizes the unmistakability there can be in knowledge which comes about by way of impressions. An example is the impossibility of confusing a passage from Chrysostom with one from Jerome; 'in each case we see the man in his language'.

It is not reason, operating on the basis of impressions, which discerns individuals in their unitary being; reason is here wholly inoperative. Nor is this discernment of the work of sense, for sense is transcended. It is the work of 'instinct'. The awareness of an external world, a world existing independently of our perception of it, is the product of 'instinctive perceptions'. And it is an 'instinct of the mind', which recognizes 'an external Master in the dictate of conscience' (p. 110).

In the previous chapter we warned ourselves of the danger of misunderstanding Newman in his use of immediacy-terms, such as 'perception', 'intuition', and 'instinct'. The danger is that of supposing him to mean that something or other is known with logical immediacy, without inferential grounds, when his point is that no inferential process is experienced. And since immediacy-terms are very frequent in Newman and can be put by him to a very surprising use (as 'perception' is, in 'Religious truth is reached, not by reasoning, but by an inward perception'), it is easy to see him as an extravagant proponent of divinatory knowledge. In fact, the likelihood is always against his claiming in any instance the existence of this sort of knowledge. The likelihood is that he sees as taking place a process of reasoning of the kind he called 'implicit', which, with its grounds merely adumbrated, its absence of logical articulation, and its unanalysable summing-up, reaches its conclusion as if this did not have to be reasoned to. Nevertheless, as we have seen, the moral sense, in his conception of it, turns out to have a logically immediate perception of right and wrong. From what we have just seen, it looks as if the 'instinct' at work in the associated contexts with which we are now concerned effects a knowledge that is similarly intuitive.[4]

In each of the three cases which Newman regards as analogous—knowledge of individuals in their unitary being, of an external world, of God through conscience—there is an

---

[4] A little paper (n.d.) 'On Counterfeit Intuitions' (Birmingham Oratory, Newman archives, A. 30. 11) shows a keen awareness of the difficulty in any claim to intuitive knowledge. The paper fails in its search for the mark of a valid intuition. The great difficulty, as Newman sees it in this paper, is with contrary intuitions. 'Thus the connection between religion and virtue is held as a first principle by Christians, yet the whole teaching of the ancient world as manifested in the manners and habits of society, denies it.' (The example shows that for Newman the intuitive can extend to a whole orientation of mind.) Our metaphysical situation—the impossibility of our comparing 'ideas' with reality—prevents any direct authentication of the intuitively apprehended. Universal or, at any rate, general agreement is mentioned as a substitute, but, obtainability apart, Newman indicates dissatisfaction with this as a criterion. A letter of his discards it as, in effect, psychologically inappropriate: for oneself claiming to know something intuitively, the criterion is unnecessary; and if I am addressing someone else, I appeal to his intuition, to how he sees the thing (Newman to H. A. Woodgate, 23 Feb. 1872; *Letters and Diaries*, xxvi. 28–9).

'instinctive' interpretation of phenomena. In the first of them there is no room at all for doubt that it is Newman's view that creatures, unable to reason, attain a knowledge of beings quite different, as single and enduring, from the phenomena by which their presence is, he says, 'signified'. The power of reasoning they lack is not just that of mere argument, but of any reasoning whatsoever, including the kind Newman calls implicit. Newman does not make the comparison, but this ability to understand what the phenomena signify has to be seen as strictly comparable to an ability to understand a language one has never learnt. Logical immediacy, then, is involved in this 'instinctive' operation. And this is no less apparent in Newman's alternative to speaking of the pheno-mena as signifying what lies beyond the reach of sense, in his saying that our warrant for taking the phenomena as evidence for this reality is 'our instinctive certitude that they are evidence' (p. 102).

Newman's view of the foundation of our belief in an 'external world' needs to be considered at greater length. By an 'external world' he means (as has commonly been meant) a physical or material world existing independently of all of our sensory experiences.

'It almost looks', Edward Sillem writes in the introductory volume to the text of Newman's *Philosophical Notebook*,

as though he was maintaining that our conviction that there exists an objective world of material realities is nothing more than a blind instinctive conviction. Such, however, was plainly not his view. In using the word 'instinct', he was (I suggest) only employing a pedestrian word to speak of what . . . many phenomenologists of today call 'the intentionality of consciousness', namely that the mind thinks in terms of real beings because its proper object is not mere sensations, but existent beings.[5]

The suggestion in this passage does not bring us closer to seeing how Newman thought we come by our belief in an

---

[5] *The Philosophical Notebook of John Henry Newman*, ed. Edward Sillem (Louvain, 1969–70), i. 188–9. A full account of the *Notebook* and of how it came to be composed is given in ch. 5 of the introductory volume to the text. Briefly, the notes—many of them papers, rather—began in 1859 as preparation for a work on the philosophy of religion which never eventuated. Material from the notes is used in the *Grammar of Assent*, which took its place.

external world. (Nor, without some development of the notion
of the intentionality of consciousness that would leave
Newman far behind, would a view be indicated less vulnerable
to dismissal on the ground that it presents this belief as a blind
conviction.) To all appearances, it is Newman's view that we
come by our belief in the existence of a material reality beyond
the impressions of sense, through 'instinctive perception', in
an operation as epistemologically mysterious as that by
which—this he certainly does maintain—we divine the
existence of individual enduring beings behind their pheno-
menal presence. Is there any reason to doubt that in
Newman's view an 'instinctive' operation of the mind takes us
from sense-impressions to our belief in a material world which
they reflect? Well, so little is done by this operation, the
content of the belief it would induce is so exiguous, as to
insinuate a doubt as to whether anything is done by it at all.

The nature of the external world (so far as we know it), left
uncharacterized in the *Grammar of Assent*, is dealt with at
length in the Letter on Matter and Spirit which (very much a
composition in draft form) was written in 1861 and is now
published as an appendix to the text of the *Philosophical
Notebook*. Early in the Letter our 'instinctive' conviction
that 'matter exists' is reduced to the conviction that 'our
impressions of things derived thro' the senses are not merely
subjective'; and this comes down to their 'betokening' their
unknown external cause or causes.[6] Instinct could hardly do
less than inform us of so little, but Newman does not here
confidently see its operation as its own sufficient warrant, and
so he recedes from speaking of the existence of matter as thus
established, to speaking of what 'the instinctive feeling of our
minds' leads us to 'assume' (p. 204).

The existence of matter established or assumed, Newman
enters upon a fuller consideration of what we know of its
nature. He reaches a common enough kind of agnosticism as
to the reality behind the phenomena of sense—along his own
path. Certain of the senses appear to invest matter with
incompatible properties. Suppose a person with only the sense
of smell. 'What would be his idea of matter?' 'I do not see',
Newman answers, 'that it would differ materially from what

[6] *Philosophical Notebook*, ii. 204–5.

we understand by spirit' (p. 206). For it would be an idea of 'something without parts', something instantaneous 'and yet entire and complete in its communication of itself'. The cause of the impressions he would consider to be 'the action of other minds on him'. Suppose him now to be endowed with sight. His conception of matter is 'revolutionized': new ideas—of extension, shape, colour, motion, whole and parts—would sweep away his old ideas of matter. In further argument for an entirely sense-relative conception of the external material world, Newman touches on the significance of the fact, disclosed by the plurality of our senses, that we might have had more senses than we do have, or altogether different ones.

The agnostic implications of the sense-relative conception of matter argued for in the Letter on Matter and Spirit are very damaging for Newman's analogy between our knowledge of the external world through sense, and of God through conscience. We have already quoted from the passage in which this analogy is stated. In full it reads:

As from a multitude of instinctive perceptions, acting in particular instances, of something beyond the senses, we generalize the notion of an external world, and then picture that world in and according to those particular phenomena from which we started, so from the perceptive power which identifies the intimations of conscience with the reverberations or echoes (so to say) of an external admonition, we proceed on to the notion of a Supreme Ruler and Judge, and then again we image Him and His attributes in those recurring intimations, out of which, as mental phenomena, our recognition of His existence was originally gained. (*Grammar of Assent*, ch. 5, § 1, p. 104)

The external world is pictured according to the phenomena of sense; but, according to the argument in the Letter on Matter and Spirit, nothing is known of it as it is in itself, nothing of what causes these phenomena.[7] Analogously, the phenomena

---

[7] Philosophical agnosticism about an external material world goes back to Newman's early thought. The following passage occurs in *The Arians of the Fourth Century*, first published in 1838, and is retained in the 4th edn. (1874): 'What are the phenomena of the external world but a divine mode of conveying to the mind the realities of existence, individuality, and the influence of being on being, the best possible, though beguiling the imagination of most men with a harmless but unfounded belief in matter as distinct from the impressions on their senses?' (ch. 1, § 3, p. 75). Newman detaches himself personally from the opinion by saying 'This at

of conscience would require something or other to be thought
of as producing them; and analogously, the warrant of instinct
may be allowed to stand for their having as their source
something external to ourselves. Analogously again, we shall
as naturally picture this according to the phenomena it
originates as we picture the material world according to the
phenomena of sense: but with as little epistemological
justification—even though no discordant suggestions come
from conscience as to the nature of the reality beyond it,
nothing corresponding to the opposite intimations (as Newman
thought) of smell and sight.

It is by a 'perceptive power'; alternatively, it is by an
'instinct of the mind' that we recognize the voice of God in the
voice of conscience. There is hardly anything for an instinct to
do in the cognitive transition from the phenomena of sense to
an external reality the nature of which is unknown. By
contrast, there is substantial work to be done in coming to a
knowledge of God from the phenomena of conscience, only it
does not seem to be done to any degree at all by instinct.
Newman proceeds from the phenomena of conscience to what,
he says, they 'imply'; he reasons from them (*Grammar of
Assent*, ch. 5, § 1). The implication is in some way casual (pp.
108–10). The feelings and other states of mind characteristic
of the activity of conscience are, essentially, 'correlative with
persons'; they are 'such as require for their exciting cause an
intelligent being'. 'If the cause of these emotions does not
belong to this visible world, the Object of his perception must
be Supernatural and Divine.' Left obscure is the nature of the
causal process involved.

In the background is a parallel between conscience and the
sense of beauty. Now, aesthetic feeling is excited by the object
itself to which it is directed, by some beauty, say, of visual
appearance. The phenomena of conscience differ from aesthetic
feeling in being always 'emotional', which aesthetic feeling is

least is the opinion of some philosophers', and leaving its truth or falsity an open
question. The existence of material substances was not theologically an open question
for Newman (as a Catholic): 'Revelation indeed teaches us the existence of such
substances'—material substances, that is (Letter on Matter and Spirit, p. 203).
There is not a trace of philosophical doubt as to their existence in a series of letters
written to Pusey in 1867, on the metaphysics of the doctrine of transubstantiation
(*Letters and Diaries*, xxiii).

only when it is 'excited by personal objects'. This difference would not affect the manner of their excitation. And the parallel between conscience and a sense of beauty at this point would impose the supposition that the phenomena of conscience have God as their immediate cause, as the beautiful object is the immediate cause of aesthetic pleasure. But this supposition does not seem compatible with God's ordinary administration of the world through secondary causes, and it seems to be cancelled when Newman puts the excitation of the emotions of which he is speaking down to *conscience* ('conscience excites all these painful emotions'). The causal inference from the phenomena of conscience to the existence of God has to be seen, then, as indirect. It will be to the effect that they can have the character they do have only if conscience has God as its creator.

Clearly, however, since Newman's primary aim is to show how a realization of God's existence is possible, he is engaged in something more than deriving theological conclusions from the phenomena of conscience. This is clear also from the occurrence of such words as 'intimation', 'discernment', 'perception', 'testimony', 'recognition' in the course of his remarks. Reasoning from the phenomena of conscience merges into something quite different. Taking its place is an evocation and a putting into words of what the phenomena of conscience 'intimate' or 'testify' to. No reasoning is involved when there is heard in the voice of conscience the reverberation of a transcendent voice. And if we cannot be brought to a recognition within ourselves of some trace of an experience of this kind when told of it, no reasoning can induce its occurrence. Given the experience, the notion of an 'instinctive perception' might be thought to be in place. But what good would it do? There is nothing about the experience that calls for it; it fills no gap in the transition of the mind from conscience to God.

Old criticism of Newman's argument for the existence of God had a causal explanation for the phenomena of conscience on which he relied, in the interiorization of human commands and prohibitions, approvals and disapprovals. We should look at a new criticism of it, which taxes it with inconsistency.

As analysed by J. L. Mackie, Newman's argument 'rests on

three premisses': the first is that conscience is to be taken 'at its face value', 'what it asserts' accepted as valid; the second is that conscience 'looks beyond the agent himself to a further imperative and a higher sanction'; the third is that 'these must stem from a person . . . if they are to arouse powerful emotions with exactly the tone of those that moral awareness involves'.[8] Endorsement of Newman's first premiss, Mackie argues, will require us to reject the other two:

If we take conscience at its face value and accept as really valid what it asserts, we must say that there is a rational prescriptivity about certain kinds of action in their own right: that they are of this or that kind is in itself a reason for doing them or for refraining from them. There is a to-be-done-ness or a not-to-be-done-ness involved *in that kind of action in itself.* If so, there is no need to look beyond this to any supernatural person who commands or forbids such action. Equally the regret, guilt, shame, and fear associated with the consciousness of having done wrong, though normally such feelings arise only in relations with persons, are in this special case natural and appropriate: what conscience, taken at its face value, tells us is that this is how one should feel about a wrong action simply in itself. That is, if we whole-heartedly accept Newman's first premiss, we must reject the second and third.

This criticism of Newman's theistic argument sees it as inconsistent over conscience at two points. First, while conscience prescribes the doing or refraining from an action because it is the kind of action it is, the argument looks beyond the action for an imperative external to it. If there is any inconsistency here, it is on the part of conscience, not of the argument; for conscience adds to its assertion of an intrinsic rightness or wrongness in the action (supposing it to make this assertion) an imperative external to the action, when it is not done, or refrained from as a matter of course. The second point at which Mackie's criticism taxes Newman's argument with inconsistency is over the phenomena of a bad conscience, in reference to which conscience is reported as telling us that 'this is how one should feel about a wrong action simply in itself'. Newman is not being challenged over what the phemonena are. And once again, if there is inconsistency, it is on the part of conscience; for while regret, guilt, and shame

[8] J. L. Mackie, *The Miracle of Theism* (Oxford, 1982), 104.

can terminate in the action itself, fear and foreboding look to its consequences for oneself.

III

. . . I must start from some first principle;—and that first principle, which I assume and shall not attempt to prove is that . . . we have by nature a conscience. (*Grammar of Assent*, ch. 5, § 1, p. 105)

It is not obvious from these words what it is that Newman is assuming. They are followed by his saying that he will 'assume, then, that Conscience has a legitimate place among our mental acts; as really so, as the action of memory, of reasoning, of imagination, or as the sense of the beautiful'. But what, in their 'legitimacy', are memory, reasoning, and imagination being contrasted with; and on what principle is the sense of the beautiful grouped with them? There is a clear pointer to Newman's meaning in supposing conscience to be a natural endowment in the following section of the *Grammar of Assent* when, looking back on this section, he says that he is not arguing 'with those who would resolve our sense of right and wrong into a sense of the Expedient or the Beautiful, or would refer its authoritiative suggestions to the effect of teaching or of association' (ch. 5, § 2, p. 123). Behind this remark is Newman's conviction that conscience is 'an original principle', 'a simple element in our nature', 'a principle planted within us, before we have had any training'.[9] It is as ingenerable as memory, reasoning, and imagination are, as underivable from what is more primitive in our constitution. It is in this respect that Newman here sees conscience and the sense of beauty as alike.

This originality of conscience is of the greatest importance for an enterprise which is to show how we can come through conscience to a belief in God. Its assumption enabled Newman, after he had said that conscience by 'its very existence carries on our minds to a Being exterior to

---

[9] *University Sermons*, No. 10, p. 183; Letter to the Duke of Norfolk, in *Difficulties Felt by Anglicans in Catholic Teaching*, ii. 248.

ourselves', to ask: 'for else, whence did it come?'[10] And if conscience is an original endowment of our nature, there will be no developmentalist account of the phenomena of conscience that will discredit any theological suggestions they might carry. This originality of conscience so important to his enterprise Newman declares that he *assumes*, assumes as 'a first principle', a start having to be made with first principles. It might be thought that some engagement with the problem of countering a developmentalist account of conscience would have presented itself to him as not less than a polemical necessity.

Developmentalist ideas permeated the Victorian intellectual atmosphere as much in the regions directly relevant to theological inference from the phenomena of conscience as anywhere. The very conception of a natual history of the sense of moral obligation threatened the foundation of any such inference. Important also were various undertakings (which some words of Newman's might vaguely indicate) to 'resolve' 'our sense of right and wrong into a sense of the Expedient'. These undertakings were to explain how in the course of time and education moral beliefs, which were utilitarian in origin, could take on the appearance of intuitive truth. The reason given by Newman in the *Grammar of Assent* for his not having to argue with those who want to resolve the sense of right and wrong into something or other, or who want to derive the authoritative character of conscience from some extraneous source, seems to bear almost no relation to the state of things at the time when he was writing: that 'conscience is the voice of God' has been acknowledged over the ages by the widest variety of minds, has 'held its ground under great intellectual and moral disadvantages', has 'ultimately triumphed in the minds of those who had rebelled' against the thought. 'Even philosophers, who have been antagonists on other points', he continues, 'agree in recognizing the inward voice of that solemn Monitor, personal, peremptory, unargumentative, irresponsible, minatory, definitive' (*Grammar of Assent*, ch. 5, § 2, pp. 122–3).

There is, however, the following note in the Proof of

---

[10] Proof of Theism, in Newman's *Philosophical Notebook*, ii. 53.

Theism (p. 60): 'it is to be considered whether this feeling of
conscience, as involving a Personal Governor is peculiar e.g.
to the Anglo-Saxons. Have the Germans it? Have the
Chinese?'[11] That Newman did not untroubledly assume the
universality of a conscience of the appropriate kind for
theological inference would make it the more surprising that
he did not undertake any argument for the originality of
conscience—if surprise is legitimate at all: it is not obvious
that a general prophylactic argument against a developmentalist account of conscience is even conceivable.[12]

To the pervasiveness in the nineteenth century of developmentalist ideas, and to the emergence of historical-mindedness,
Newman himself had made an early and unique contribution
in his *Essay on the Development of Doctrine*. (Lord Acton said
of the *Essay* that it 'did more than any other book' of
Newman's time 'to make his countrymen think historically,
and watch the process as well as the result'.)[13] The transition

[11] Newman's impression of Chinese culture made it anomalously significant to him
from the point of view of religion. Chinese culture is mentioned in a sermon, preached
in 1873, fraught with foreboding over a new kind of world Christianity was entering
upon: 'Christianity has never yet had experience of a world simply irreligious.
Perhaps China may be an exception. We do not know enough about it to speak, but
consider what the Roman and Greek world was when Christianity appeared. It was
full of superstition, not of infidelity' ('The Infidelity of the Future', in *Catholic
Sermons of Cardinal Newman* (London, 1957), 123–4). These sermons, previously
unpublished, were edited with an introduction by Charles Stephen Dessain, at the
Birmingham Oratory.

[12] Newman was fully aware that in assuming that we have by nature a conscience,
he was assuming what would not be conceded by a great deal of contemporary
opinion. 'You will say'. he writes in one of his letters, 'that the 19th century does not
believe in conscience.' But something must be assumed, 'and in assuming conscience I
assume what is least to assume, what most will admit' (Newman to William Robert
Brownlow, 13 Apr. 1870; *Letters and Diaries*, xxv. 97). Newman, however, puts a
misplaced emphasis upon our having by nature a conscience. His primary assumption
is that the deliverances of conscience validly point beyond themselves. Given that
assumption, conscience is certainly not a mere product of society and our upbringing.
And that assumption the deliverances of conscience impose upon us, if his description
of their character is correct. A brief remark in the *Grammar of Assent* diminishes
slightly the isolated appearance of his conviction that conscience is an original
endowment of human nature, by giving it some foundation in the experienced
character of conscience: 'if there be those who deny that the dictate of conscience is
ever more than a taste, or an association, it is a less difficulty to me to believe that they
are deficient either in the religious sense or in their memory of early years, than that
they never had at all what those around them without hesitation profess to have
received from nature' (ch. 5, § 2, pp. 123–4).

[13] Quoted by Hugh A. Macdougall from one of the Acton MSS in Cambridge
University Library, in *The Acton-Newman Relations* (New York, 1962), 154.

he conducts from conscience to the existence and attributes of God reflects nothing of the nineteenth century. Conceptually, it could have belonged to the eighteenth century, and have been the work of Butler.

IV

In Newman's phenomenology of conscience we are made to feel the otherness of conscience from ourselves. In the experience to which Newman draws our attention we do not seem to be addressing ourselves in the dictate of conscience, nor to be passing judgement on ourselves when our conscience condemns us. At the same time, the experience is, of course, quite unlike being ordered to do something by someone else, and being condemned by someone else for what we have done. How does Newman conceive of the structural relation between one's conscience and one's self? The incidental discussion of conscience as a faculty at the beginning of the previous chapter indicated an answer: that certain acts and states of oneself are one's conscience. But the question needs to be resumed now that conscience as a dictate is under consideration, for Newman was thinking of conscience as that when he said that conscience is 'more than a man's own self'.

Though Newman often evokes in a reader a sense of the mystery of conscience, it is never by the suggestion of ontological mystery in the nature of conscience; in particular, his idea of conscience is altogether free of the notion that conscience is something within us with a hidden being and agency. No doubt, what might seem in a writer to be an entitative conception of conscience is, much more often than not, merely unreflected upon metaphor. So for a contrast against which to set the view to be elicited from Newman, we shall take a writer whose entitative conception of conscience is one of theory—Freud.

The suggestion of another within oneself, which lies at the origin of the word 'conscience', has an almost literal equivalent in Freud's theory:

let us dwell for a moment on the view which the melancholic's disorder affords of the constitution of the human ego. We see how in him one part of the ego sets itself over against the other, judges it critically, and, as it were, takes it as its object . . . What we are here becoming acquainted with is the agency commonly called 'conscience'.[14]

In Freud's final topography of the mind conscience is a 'function' of the super-ego, which is an agency with an independent existence within the ego, resulting from separation from the ego.[15] Observation of the ego is another function of the super-ego; the holding up of exacting standards to the ego yet another.

Our concern with Freud was to obtain some statement of an entitative conception of conscience for contrast with Newman's non-entitative one, but two other matters are worth noticing before to go on to look at Newman's conception. Freud eminently provides an illustration of the developmentalist threat to theological inference from the phenomena of conscience. There is, Freud maintained, 'psychological truth' in the thought of conscience as having a divine origin: 'The same father (or parental agency) which gave the child life and guarded him against its perils, taught him as well what he might do and what he must leave undone, instructed him that he must adapt himself to certain restrictions on his instinctual wishes.' Depersonalized, the prohibitions and commands of his parents endure in the grown man as his conscience. And the father, life-giver and protector, clothed 'with all the magnificence in which he once appeared to the small child', becomes the heavenly Father.[16]

[14] 'Mourning and Melancholia' (1915), *Freud's Works* (Standard edn.; London, 1953–74) xiv. 247.
[15] *New Introductory Lectures on Psycho-Analysis* (1933), lect. 31; *Works*, xxii. 59–60. Freud warns against too sharp a differentiation of the structures of the personality: 'In thinking of this division of the personality into an ego, a super-ego and an id, you will not, of course, have pictured sharp frontiers like the artificial ones drawn in political geography' (p. 79).
[16] *New Introductory Lectures*, lect. 35, pp. 163–4. Freud's account of the origin of theistic religion is the telling of a story rather than the setting up of an explanatory theory with empirical implications that might be confirmed or falsified. (Moore reports Wittgenstein as saying in connection with Freud's account of laughter: 'what he says sounds as if it were science when in fact it is only a "wonderful representation" '; G. E. Moore, 'Wittgenstein's Lectures in 1930–35', in *Philosophical Papers* (London, 1959), 316). In contrast with a question asking whether an account, such as Freud's, of the origin of theistic religion is true, to ask whether the 'Chinese' have a conscience sufficiently similar to the one Freud and Newman knew, to allow

Also worth noticing when Freud's views are brought into juxtaposition with Newman's is the severity of conscience in their characterization of it.[17] Freud's characterization of conscience has close affinities with Greek feeling about conscience. Orestes was tortured by his conscience for an unintentional crime; Freud has conscience punishing for wishes that never become formed intentions. We have already seen that for Newman dark emotions predominate when conscience is in operation. Late in the *Grammar of Assent* (ch. 10, § 1, pp. 390–1), discussing natural religion as a preparation for revealed religion, he says of conscience that conveying a sense of God as before all else a Judge dealing out retributive justice, 'its effect is to burden and sadden the religious mind'. (Nothing could be more remote from the euphoric engaged-in-protest conscience, which became so pronounced a feature of the Western religious mind in recent times, than conscience as characterized by Newman—except conscience as characterized by Freud.)

Elements of an ontology of conscience are among the preliminaries to the theistic argument in the Proof of Theism. (There is nothing of significance in the theistic argument itself which is not reproduced in the *Grammar of Assent*.) The preliminaries are largely concerned with what comes within the scope of consciousness as contrasted with what does not. 'I am conscious of my own existence.'[18] This seems to mean, in the light of what follows, that I am conscious of myself as the subject of various states of mind (such-and-such a feeling, for instance), and of myself as agent in various actions. My consciousness of myself as subject and agent is 'indirect', coming about by way of a consciousness of my states of mind and actions, of which consciousness is 'direct'. Doubt can get no footing against that of which one is conscious. Once a philosophical commonplace, this principle is rendered more opaque than it already is by Newman's distinction between direct and indirect consciousness. Newman applies the principle of the indubitability of that of which one is conscious in a

Newman's argument its data, does seem to be a question capable of an empirical answer.

[17] For Freud on this matter see especially *Civilization and its Discontents* (1933).
[18] *Philosophical Notebook* ii. 31.

contrast between certain kinds of sensation, on the one hand, and the material objects whose presence is intimated by these sensations, on the other: that the sensation exists has the guarantee of consciousness; that the material object exists does not (though the 'persuasion' that it exists does).

Conscience has so far made a very unobstrusive appearance in these preliminaries, as 'a certain feeling on my mind'. As this feeling, its existence, like that of our sensations, will have the guarantee of consciousness, but any testimony it might give to something beyond itself would be as unratified by consciousness as any testimony of the sort given by any of our sensations. Unaccountably, however, Newman writes:

What is internal to the mind is an object of consciousness which external things are not. Thus the line is broad and deep between reliance on reason or conscience and upon the trustworthiness of the impressions of the senses or the reality . . . of matter. Hence the being of a God, arising out of what is internal, is an external fact different in evidence . . . from every other external fact.[19] (p. 41)

So far as they are 'objects of consciousness', reason (that is, reasoning) and conscience are no more than psychological occurrences; consciousness therefore will be altogether neutral as regards any trustworthiness in their deliverances.

We need one more thing from these preliminaries before we can summarize Newman's view of the manner of being which conscience has, and at the same time his conception of the relation of one's conscience to oneself. Newman lists among the 'primary conditions of the mind which are involved in the fact of [one's] existence': memory, sensation, reasoning, and conscience. He explains that in speaking of these conditions he is speaking of the 'mind in its several modes, viz. the mind feeling, the mind remembering, the mind reasoning &c.' (pp. 43, 45). There is something which might be worth noticing incidentally here. It is just possible that Newman was induced to feel that a developmentalist conception of conscience was blocked by the very nature of conscience as being one of the 'conditions' of a person's existence. The language invites the

[19] It is likely that Newman himself came to repudiate the position taken up in this passage, for there is no trace of it in the *Grammar of Assent*, where, on the contrary, the phenomena of conscience and the impressions of the senses are placed entirely on a level as regards their witness to what lies beyond them.

illusion. For illusion it certainly is. I am conscious of my self
only with and by way of some one of other of its operations or
mental states, Newman maintains, in language which confers
upon these modes an ambiguous essentiality to my existence:
they are 'conditions' of it, 'part of the initial idea' of it, 'bound
up in my "I am" '. This makes them sound as if they were
constitutive of my being, and if conscience is that, it cannot
be the product of my upbringing. In fact, all that is essential
here is a modal side to my being, and this requirement is
satisfied by modes, the most ephemeral and adventitious.
That of course was obvious to Newman. Still, this way of
speaking might have prompted a tendency to think of
conscience as ingenerable when it is viewed (along with
reason, sense, and memory) in a faculty-manner, disposition-
ally, and not in its actualization as 'a certain feeling on my
mind'.

Any notion of conscience as an occult entity is not only
absent from the materials we have assembled from the
preliminaries in the Proof of Theism, but excluded by them.
There is nothing occult in the activity of conscience—this lies
open before consciousness; there is only one entity involved in
this activity—oneself. One's conscience is oneself thinking in
certain ways and being subject to feelings of certain kinds. If a
distinction is made between one's conscience and oneself, the
manner of being of conscience is entirely modal, like that of
sensations or feelings or any other of our states of mind.
Viewed in a faculty-manner, conscience is no more other than
oneself than one's reason is or one's senses are.

How, then, are we to understand Newman's remark that
conscience is 'more than a man's own self'? What follows this
remark in the sermon in which it occurs, and is quoted in the
Proof of Theism, explains it in a way fully compatible with the
account given in the Proof of Theism of the manner of being
possessed by conscience:

The man himself has not power over it, or only with extreme
difficulty; he did not make it, he cannot destroy it. He may silence it
in particular cases or directions; he may distort its enunciations;
but he cannot, or it is quite the exception if he can, he cannot
emancipate himself from it.[20]

[20] *Sermons on Various Occasions* (1857), No. 5, pp. 64–5.

The analogy to suggest itself is one which brings conscience
again into the strong association it has in Newman with sense.
The analogy is with the involuntariness of sense-experience.

V

An 'infallible guide of conduct, a sort of deity within us'.
Neither of the descriptions in this fragment of the *Oxford
English Dictionary*'s summary of a range of opinion about
conscience would be allowed by Newman. A guide of conduct
Newman indeed thought conscience was, but not an infallible
one. Infallibility within a certain sphere is assigned to
conscience in a comment (dated 9 May 1868) on the
contention in the Proof of Theism that the dictate of
conscience testifies to its 'divine origin': 'It may be asked, How
can an oracle be divine which is not infallible in its answers?
But conscience errs not in principles, but in details. There is
always something true in its dictates.'[21] Nothing of this
comment is reproduced in the *Grammar of Assent*, where it is
the magisterial character of the dictate of conscience, in this
respect 'one and the same in the mind of every one', which
betokens its divine origin. But being infallible in the apprehension of moral principles would not make conscience an
infallible guide of life, least of all for Newman, for whom the
guidance of conscience is to be experienced (and, by fidelity to
it, refined) in the particularity of actual situations.[22]

No one is cited by the *Dictionary* as sponsoring the opinion
that conscience is an infallible guide of conduct. This is not to
be wondered at. Let it be supposed that conscience determines
right and wrong, and since more than generalities are needed
for the guidance of conduct, let it be supposed further that its
declarations are not (or not only) moral platitudes, but are as
particular as the situations in which right and wrong have to
be determined. Now, as everyone knows, the judgements

---

[21] *Philosophical Notebook*, ii. 58.

[22] The particularity of conscience apart, there is a difficulty to be noticed in at once
having conscience inerrant in moral principles and holding that, as it is said in the
Grammar of Assent (ch. 1, § 4, p. 65), these principles are 'really conclusions or
abstractions from particular experiences' of right and wrong. Infallibility in this
abstractive procedure would be a very remarkable endowment.

people make as to the moral requirements of particular situations are often rejected by others. If these judgements are going to be said to proceed from conscience, then we have the declarations of one person's conscience often contradicted by those of someone else's conscience. Further, a person sometimes comes to regard an earlier moral judgement of his own as mistaken—his 'conscience' at one time is contradicted by his 'conscience' at another. These are the facts which make it very improbable that anyone given to reflection could hold the opinion that conscience is an infallible guide of conduct. It is, therefore, worth looking at what has every appearance of being an assertion of this opinion.

'Divine instinct', Rousseau apostrophizes conscience,

immortal voice from heaven; sure guide for a creature ignorant and finite indeed, yet intelligent and free; infallible judge of good and evil, making man like to God.[23]

There are problems sometimes in getting at Rousseau's meaning when he speaks about conscience. A difficulty is inconsistency in his language. Thus, a few pages after the apostrophe to conscience, conscience is assigned an affective role in relation to right and wrong; 'reason' has the cognitive role—'Has he not given me conscience that I may love the right, reason that I may perceive it?' (p. 257). But this reason which does not seem to be ratiocinative, unlike the calculating reason which Rousseau pointedly distinguishes from conscience, seems to be conscience in all but name. Rousseau earlier warned that the words he used would not always have the same meaning, their context providing 'a sort of definition' (bk. 2, p. 72). Shifts in the meaning of words whose relationship to one another is important, and an extravagant tone, do not, however, diminish the appearance that infallibility is ascribed to conscience: an infallibility not confined to general principles of conduct. A casuist deals with right and wrong in particular cases, and conscience is a 'casuist':

I find them [the principles of conduct] in the depths of my heart traced by nature in characters which nothing can efface. I need only consult myself with regard to what I wish to do; what I feel to be right is right, what I feel to be wrong is wrong; conscience is the best

[23] *Émile* (1780), bk. 4 ('Profession de foi du vicaire savoyard'), Everyman edn. (London, 1911), p. 254.

casuist; and it is only when we haggle with conscience that we have recourse to the subtleties of argument . . . conscience never deceives us; she is the true guide of man . . . he who obeys his conscience is following nature and he need not fear that he will go astray. (pp. 249–50)

There is a device which would protect the idea of an infallible conscience from simple annihilation by the colliding judgements on right and wrong made by different persons, and by the same person at different times. It is to have conscience speak infallibly, but not to inerrant hearing. The voice of conscience is heard, Rousseau says (at the end of the *Discours sur les sciences et les artes*) in the 'silence of the passions', and with the mind clear of prejudice. These criteria for identifying the voice of conscience, for distinguishing it from its simulation, are, however, insufficient, since, to all telling, the minds of those in contradiction over some matter of right and wrong can be equally clear of passion and prejudice. And significant improvement upon them seems impossible. If there are no criteria which will identify declarations of conscience from simulated declarations of conscience, in differences over right and wrong, the notion of an infallible conscience is altogether idle.

Let us return to the passages from Rousseau which seem to incorporate this notion. The mention of one's haggling with conscience in the second passage implies a situation in which the rightness or wrongness of an action does not have to be determined because it is not really in question; I am disingenuously 'having recourse to the subtleties of argument'. Applied to this situation, the words 'what I feel to be right is right' express an injunction to oneself to avoid self-deception, not an enunciation of the principle to be adopted in ascertaining the right thing to do. The meaning of the second passage would not, however, be exhausted by an interpretation controlled by the notion of haggling with conscience; at the beginning and end of the quotation conscience guides the sincere. And that interpretation leaves an understanding of the first passage untouched. But it prompts an understanding of both passages as concerned with the virtue of the agent rather than with the rightness of an action. Both passages might just be able to bear the strain of being construed so as to have

conscience an infallible guide, not to the rightness or
wrongness of actions, but to action with the right disposition,
an infallible guide, therefore, in the path of virtue. On this
understanding, though, conscience would be misleadingly
described as infallible. On this understanding, the infallibility
of conscience becomes a never-failing rule for our guidance:
follow conscience.

We shall use ideas in this understanding of Rousseau to
approach the problem facing Newman, raised by his question
'How can an oracle be divine which is not infallible in its
answers?' How can conscience be the voice of God, unless its
deliverances are infallible? It might be thought that the
question does not arise for Newman because for him
conscience speaks as God's representative in its commands
and prohibitions. For the question as to the infallibility of
something or other even to arise, it might be argued, it has to
be supposed that it issues declarations which are, in themselves, apart from the exercise of infallibility, capable of being
either true or false; and just as ordinary commands and
prohibitions are not of this type, so neither are the imperatival
utterances of conscience. Now, infallibility can be restricted,
as it is by the Church which claims it, to teaching, to what is to
be believed, and given no application to the commands and
prohibitions of ecclesiastical administration and policy. But
this narrowing down is no help with Newman's problem.
Without restriction, to be infallible is never to err. If you
command what is wrong, you have erred in your command.
And when conscience is regarded as speaking as God's
representative, for it to command what is wrong is as bad as it
would be for it to tell us something false.

This might meet the difficulty: When God commands
through conscience, He does not command the doing of x
simply, but of x-seen-as-right; because only by doing this will
one act with the right disposition. God does not err in his
command; conscience errs, but not in a way incompatible with
its voicing the command of God.

In the second of the two descriptions of conscience linked
together in the *Oxford English Dictionary* conscience is 'a sort
of deity within us'. Newman would not, of course, have God
degraded to a sort of deity. In his novel *Callista* (set in the

third century), he does, however, have Callista say, 'I feel that God within my heart', and the reference is clearly to conscience.[24] But this is only a way of speaking, and an exceptional one in Newman. (He has Callista go on to say: 'You may tell me that this dictate is a mere law of my nature. . . . No, it is the echo of a person speaking to me.') Newman will deliberately modify the supreme conscience-metaphor to make conscience not the voice of God, but its 'echo' or 'reverberation'. There is no place in his thought for anything supernatural in the being of conscience; ontologically, conscience is no more to be distinguished from oneself than one's reason is. Bremond's assertion, quoted near the beginning of this essay, that Newman's whole philosophy is aimed at establishing 'a fundamental identity between the voice of conscience and the voice of God', belongs to the rhetoric of commentary on Newman.

We have looked in this section at the notion of conscience as an infallible guide of conduct without picking up anything that would explain how so empty a notion could originate. In fact, a plausible explanation lies at hand—in a spurious implication of the metaphor in which conscience is the voice of God. Let the metaphor have come into existence, and let conscience be unreflectingly thought of as determining right and wrong: how naturally it will be thought of as infallible, being *that* voice. The transition suggested in the *Dictionary*'s arrangement of the two descriptions of conscience which we have considered is the other way round: from an 'infallible guide of conduct' to 'a sort of deity within us'. There is no quotation ascribing infallibility to conscience. But, as it happens, the second of these phrases echoes a phrase from one of the quotations the *Dictionary* has gathered. In this quotation what conscience does is not anything which summons up the idea of infallibility; what it does is prohibit and threaten:

> I feel not
> This deity in my bosom: twenty consciences,
> That stand 'twixt me and Milan, candied be they,
> And melt, ere they molest!
> (*The Tempest* 2. 1. 278 ff.)

[24] *Callista* (1855), ch. 28, p. 314.

An effect of Newman's phenomenology of conscience is to make one realize how naturally conscience should come to be called the voice of God, without either the ascription of infallibility to any of its operations, or the assumption that it is God dwelling within us.

VI

The conscience which Newman saw as making available to us a realization of the existence of God and of our individual relation to God as ruler and judge is altogether ordinary. It has no being which transcends our own, and the experiences we undergo when it is at work, with their intimations of what is beyond ourselves, are (unlike those which mystics report) everyday experiences. At no point in the transition Newman conducts from conscience to God is there any departure from the conception implicit in the functioning of the word 'conscience' in its natural, proper, unextended use. This use of the word does not, of course, have theistic implications. The theistic implications and intimations of conscience which Newman aims at having us recognize are not conceptual ones. Their source is experience. They are derived from the phenomena of conscience—of conscience strictly so called, conscience in 'the ordinary sense of the word', not of something that has been given its name.

In all three chapters of this essay we have been considering the nature of conscience, what conscience is and does; in the first chapter the nature of conscience in the ordinary conception of it, in the second and third chapters the nature of conscience in Newman's conception of it. In Newman's conception, conscience determines the rightness or wrongness of actions in the concrete situations in which we find ourselves, and in doing this it is able to engage in reasoning. If the account that has been given of the ordinary conception of conscience is substantially correct, conscience undertakes no determination of right and wrong and engages in no reasoning. If this account of conscience is correct, and if the 'magisterial aspect' of conscience is taken to cover the accusatory or condemnatory operation of conscience as well as its imperatival operation, then in describing this 'aspect' of conscience, Newman has described conscience in its entirety.

In the following chapter we shall see conscience brought by Newman into relationship with the authority of the Church —conscience with both the aspects he took it to have, determinative as well as magisterial. Obviously, in this relationship there are possibilities of conflict. Newman, as we shall see, attempted to show the impossibility of a *deadlocked* conflict, by a separation of domains, in one of which the word of ecclesiastical authority is final, in the other the word of conscience. The particularity of all of the dictates delivered by conscience is an essential element in his argument. And it is essential that conscience should be able to reason if it is to have credibility, let alone authority, in its clash with ecclesiastical authority.

In the notion of conscience as having authority we come upon a feature of Newman's conception of conscience which we have not considered so far. It is an important notion, and much more opaque than it might appear. It could not be given satisfactory consideration abstracted from the setting in which we shall find it placed by Newman in the following chapter. How Newman's ascription of authority to conscience is to be understood, and upon what grounds authority might be ascribed to conscience, are questions taken up incidentally in this chapter and centrally in Chapter 5.

The ecclesiastical authority into relationship with which conscience is brought by Newman is primarily papal authority. This is a consequence of the historial occasion of his one piece of writing on the subject which runs to any extent, the Letter to the Duke of Norfolk. As everyone knows who has heard Newman's views on conscience mentioned, he said that in an after-dinner toast he would drink to conscience first and then to the pope.[25] We shall try to see what is to be made of this remark.

[25] Letter to the Duke of Norfolk, § 5, in *Difficulties of Anglicans,* ii. 261.

4

DOMAINS OF AUTHORITY

I

In 1870 the First Vatican Council defined the infallibility of the pope as an article of faith. In 1874 Gladstone brought out The Vatican Decrees in their Bearing on Civil Allegiance: a Political Expostulation, in which he maintained that the Vatican decrees had put the conscience of every Catholic at the pope's disposal. The pope claims to be infallible in both faith and morals, and, Gladstone contended, there are no 'departments and functions of human life which do not and cannot fall within the domain of morals' (Expostulation, p. 36). But wider still than the reach of infallibility is the claim to an 'absolute and entire Obedience' (p. 37). On 'all matters respecting which any Pope may think proper to declare that they concern either faith, or morals, or the government or discipline of the Church', 'absolute obedience' is claimed from every member of the Church (p. 42). And by no 'acknowledged or intelligible line' are these domains which the pope appropriates separated from the domains of civil duty and allegiance (p. 45). Newman replied to Gladstone in A Letter to the Duke of Norfolk (1875).

Conscience and papal infallibility are brought into relationship in the Letter after Newman has discussed the indeterminate domain which Gladstone saw as opened up, 'not indeed to the abstract assertion of Infallibility', but to the 'practical and decisive demand of Absolute Obedience' (Expostulation, p. 41). Newman treats the expression 'absolute obedience' with irony—Gladstone 'speaks of "*absolute obedience*" so often, that any reader . . . would think that the word "absolute" was the Pope's word, not his' (Letter, §4, p. 233); but just because it is Gladstone's word, Newman

sometimes uses it himself. And upon the meaning he attaches
to it depends our understanding of his denial that absolute
obedience is due to the pope. The passage of the Council's
decree, upon which Gladstone was drawing, provides no
indirect assistance as to what might be meant by 'absolute
obedience'. With regard to papal jurisdiction, the decree lays it
down that clergy and people are 'bound by the duty of
hierarchical subordination and true obedience,[1] not only in
matters which pertain to faith and morals, but also in those
which pertain to the discipline and regimen of the Church'.
The domain envisaged, as Newman points out, is ecclesiastical,
not that of human conduct in general; the pope is not being
given 'general authority over us in all things whatsoever'
(Letter, pp. 233 ff).

Absolute obedience can be due neither to the pope nor to
the State, Newman maintains in the following passage:

When . . . Mr. Gladstone asks Catholics how they can obey the
Queen and yet obey the Pope, since it may happen that the
commands of the two authorities may clash, I answer, that it is my
rule, both to obey the one and to obey the other, but that there is no
rule in this world without exceptions, and if either the Pope or the
Queen demanded of me an 'Absolute Obedience,' he or she would be
trangressing the laws of human nature and human society. I give an
absolute obedience to neither. Further, if ever this double allegiance
pulled me in contrary ways, which in this age of the world I think it
never will, then I should decide according to the particular case,
which is beyond all rule, and must be decided on its own merits.
(Letter, p. 243)

The meaning of 'absolute obedience' in this passage is clear. It
is obedience which is unlimited in extent, obedience to
whatever might be commanded. We shall come presently to a
passage in which it does not have this meaning.

On the issue of double allegiance Newman is a particularist.
Supposing parliament to enact a law requiring Catholic
attendance at Protestant services and the pope to forbid this
attendance, he would obey the pope. (The example is perhaps
intended to play its part obliquely in conveying a sense of the

---

[1] Denzinger, *Enchiridion Symbolorum*, No. 1827: '. . . officio hierarchicae
subordinationis veraeque oboedientiae obstringuntur . . .'. The translation is
Newman's.

anachronistic character of the fears Gladstone was arousing, as
well as being as accusing reminder of the past.) If, in the
event of the Prince of Wales turning Catholic, the pope were
to pronounce Catholic members of parliament released from
their oath to maintain the Protestant Succession and to call on
them to back up the right of the Prince, Newman, were he one
of them, would disobey the pope. More interestingly, were the
pope to require British Catholics in the armed services to
refuse to fight in a certain war, Newman, supposing himself
involved, would refuse to obey the pope if he could not
himself see the war as unjust. Every case must be decided on
its merits: altogether unobtainable is the 'intelligible line'
demanded by Gladstone between papal and civil jurisdiction.
But there is no menace to civil jurisdiction in this fact. How
are collisions managed between co-ordinate civil powers? Not
in the ordinary run of things by war. There are 'conferences,
compromises, arbitrations'. In such cases 'neither party gives
up its abstract rights, but neither party practically insists on
them . . . Neither party says "I will not make it up with you,
till you draw an intelligible line between your domain and
mine" ' (p. 237).

As for the bearing of papal jurisdiction on the everyday life
of Catholics, there is hardly any, in fact. 'Mr. Gladstone says
that "the Pontiff declares to belong to him the *supreme
direction* of Catholics in respect to all duty".' 'Supreme
direction; true, but "supreme" is not "minute," nor does
"direction" mean "supervision" or "management" ', Newman
begins his comment (p. 227). In the analogy then drawn
between the bearing of papal jurisdiction on a person's life and
the bearing of the law upon it, absolute obedience is
mentioned. The expression does not have the same meaning as
in the passage previously quoted.

Take the parallel of human law; the Law is *supreme,* and the Law
directs our conduct under the manifold circumstances in which we
have to act, and may and must be absolutely obeyed; but who
therefore says that the Law has the 'supreme direction' of us? The
State, as well as the Church, has the power at its will of imposing
laws upon us, laws bearing on our moral duties, our daily conduct,
affecting our actions in various ways, and circumscribing our
liberties; yet no one would say that the Law, after all, with all its

power in the abstract and its executive vigour in fact, interferes either with our comfort or our conscience. (p. 227)

'Absolute obedience' in the passage previously quoted is obedience which is unlimited in extent, compliance with absolutely anything which a given authority chooses to stipulate. Here it seems to mean compliance to the letter with what is legitimately stipulated. When Newman denied that 'absolute obedience' was due either to the pope or to the State, he did not mean that neither was ever entitled to simple obedience.[2]

In the course of the discussion of colliding jurisdictions, in an incidental remark, the authority of the pope is said to be 'not "absolute" even in religious matters, as Mr. Gladstone would have it to be', but to have, 'a supreme call on our obedience' (p. 240). This time one has to cast about for an explanation of the limit placed on papal authority in its not being 'absolute'. Newman may have had in mind prescriptive or procedural checks on what a pope can do. But a consideration of an altogether different kind might lie behind the remark. He will be maintaining further on in the Letter to the Duke of Norfolk that obedience to the injunctions of a pope, for all their vast authority in religious matters, must be withheld at the dictate of conscience.

So far we have been concerned with the jurisdictional authority of the pope and with papal injunctions, not with the doctrinal authority of the pope and papal teaching. It is a papal injunction that the dictate of conscience will override. The possibility of an encounter between conscience and teaching—teaching, in particular, conceived of as having a claim to infallibility behind it—has not yet come into view. As a step towards our considerations of Newman's treatment of this matter, which lies well ahead, we shall be looking in the

---

[2] In a letter to Gladstone written some years after the controversy Newman speaks of the power of the pope as 'absolute' within a certain domain. Gladstone had hoped that just possibly through Newman (now a cardinal) the pope might be induced to curb the rebellious utterances of Irish priests. 'I think you overrate the Pope's power in political and social matters,' Newman wrote. 'It is absolute in questions of theology, but not so in practical matters.' The power, rather than the authority, of the pope is being emphasized in the letter. His action in practical matters is 'only in the long run effective . . . local power or influence is often more than a match for Roman right'. (Newman to Gladstone, 23 Dec. 1881; *Letters and Diaries*, xxx. 36–7.)

next section at his treatment of the notion of 'private judgement'.

Newman was aware of the necessity that the claim he makes for conscience in relation to papal authority be consistent with a Catholic position; Gladstone's charges could not be given a Protestant answer. Before we leave the subject of absolute obedience, however, we should notice a contention that a development of his thought on that subject shows up the illusoriness of the division between Catholic and Protestant over private judgement.

'For Newman . . . if we may extend and develop his thought', Max Charlesworth writes,

the pope's authority and power cannot be so absolute that it admits of no possible abuse; and the authority and sovereignty of the state cannot be so absolute that it admits of no possible abuse. And therefore the dichotomy between the Catholic's appeal to the absolute authority of the pope and the Protestant's appeal to 'conscience' or private judgment is an illusory one. For the Catholic's obedience to the pope cannot be a blind and irrational act as though he said 'I will do whatever—literally and strictly whatever—the Pope tells me to do, without question' . . . If by an act of the will, I surrender, wholly and without any reservation, the power of making subsequent acts of will, then those acts cease to be *mine* and to be morally imputable to me. In this sense 'absolute obedience', if we take this in its strict and literal sense, is not a moral posture at all. In the last resort, it is my own act of 'conscience', my own judgment and decision about what I ought to do, which is 'absolute'; for an act is only mine, and only a moral act, in so far as it issues from my own judgment and decision about what is good and bad.[3]

In the course of this passage 'absolute obedience' changes its meaning. At first, as corresponding to an authority which cannot be abused because there is nothing outside its province, it is obedience which is unlimited in extent, obedience holding whatever the word of command might be. It would have as its contrast obedience within certain areas. At the end of the passage, absolute obedience is contrasted with deciding for oneself what to do, forming one's own judgement about what is good and bad —contrasted, therefore, with what is not obedience at all.

[3] Max Charlesworth, *Church, State and Conscience* (St Lucia, Queensland, 1973), 30.

The unfolding of Newman's thought in the course of this passage would have astonished him. In place of an external authority with the final say on any matter it allocates to itself is set the judgement, similarly unrestricted in scope, in matters with a moral complexion, of everyone's 'conscience'. Subject to this verdict-giving judgement are matters belonging to the area in which Newman thought the Church spoke with finality, in which he saw private judgement on the part of someone professing to belong to the Church as, logically, an intruder—the area known as that of 'faith and morals'. Now, it might be objected that the intention of the writer of the passsage has been misrepresented, that in his expository development of Newman's thought there is no reference to this area. And as ground for the objection, it might be pointed out that all through the passage (as the context in Newman required), it is actions that are spoken of and, correspondingly, papal injunctions; never matters of belief and, correspondingly, teaching. Contrary to the objection, it is over matters of belief that the dichotomy exists between the Catholic's appeal to authority and the Protestant's to private judgement. But whatever the writer's intention, his development of Newman's thought renders it inconsistent, for out of this development comes a proposition incompatible with the existence of part of the area in which Newman saw the Church as having absolute authority: 'an act is only mine, and only a moral act, in so far as it issues from my own judgment and decision about what is good and bad'. If this unargued-for proposition is true, there can be no moral beliefs which any authority could impose.

II

Presupposed by the notion of what came to be called 'private judgement' is the notion of a divine revelation, the revelation in which Catholicism and Protestantism alike professed belief. The most fundamental difference between them is over the way in which we are to ascertain the content of this revelation. Involved in this difference is disagreement over the use of private judgement.

Thinking out as an Anglican a Catholic conception of the Church, Newman had reached the ideas on private judgement that were to remain with him for the rest of his life by the time he wrote the essay 'Private Judgment' in 1841.[4] Written within four years of his conversion to Roman Catholicism, its general concern is with the 'fearful issue' of a change in religion. A change of religion results from an act of private judgement. The essay (which ends by adducing considerations aimed at showing that an Anglican need not change his religion) raises first a difficulty about private judgement. This difficulty is that private judgement leads various minds in very different directions and yet the presupposition of its use is that there is an ascertainable truth. With this difficulty moral questions about private judgement start up. How can it be the duty its advocates proclaim? Is it good only 'under circumstances, and with limitations'? Or perhaps, considering the disturbance it creates, not good at all?

Newman goes to Scripture for guidance as to the right exercise of private judgement. What he finds sanctioned by its precedents is not enquiry 'about Gospel doctrine, but about the Gospel teacher'; not enquiry aimed at determining what God has revealed, but enquiry as to who it is that God has commissioned ('Private Judgment', § 3, p. 350). The use of private judgement which has Scriptural warrant is enquiry into the credentials of a teacher. Newman goes on to say that this view of the domain of private judgement harmonizes both

---

[4] Now in *Essays Critical and Historical*, ii, to which the page numbers refer. Private judgement is a very substantial topic in *The Prophetical Office of the Church* (1837), but it is difficult to make out one important part of what is being said, and difficult as well to know what to make of the view as a whole. Teaching the 'doctrine of the Apostles', the Church as a province separate from that of private judgement. The reason given for this separation of provinces has, however, the appearance of being a reason for their coincidence. Teaching the doctrine of the Apostles, the Church teaches 'what is an historical fact, and ascertainable as other facts, and obvious to the intelligence of inquirers . . . and Private Judgment has as little exercise here as in any matters of sense or experience. It may as well claim a right of denying that the Apostles existed.' As Newman continues, however, it becomes clear that he is thinking of private judgement as occupied with what is speculative or matter of opinion, as opposed to matter of fact ascertainable by enquiry. But what the Church teaches seems no longer to be matter of fact ascertainable by enquiry: the Church has authority in doctrinal controversies, and if this authority depends on 'the mere knowledge of an historical fact', 'any individual of competent information has the same in his place and degree' (*The Prophetical Office of the Church*, lect. 8, § 1, § 3 (3rd edn., 1877), in *The Via Media*, i. 189–91).

with the nature of religion and with the actualities of human life. 'Religion is for practice and that immediate' (p. 353). The ratiocinative processes needed to elicit doctrines from the Scriptures are 'slow' and 'cold'. And the great mass of people, which has neither the time nor the desire to engage in them, is much better able to judge of persons or 'bodies or men' than of 'propositions'. Of course, private judgement may err even within its proper domain. Those who 'think they have, in consequence of their inquiries, found the teacher of truth, may be wrong in the result they have arrived at; but those who despise the notion of a teacher altogether, are already wrong before they begin them' (p. 356).

That the proper use of private judgement is in examination of the credentials of a teacher claiming a divine mission is a point made in the following passage written many years later; but its main point is the incoherence of accepting the teacher and subjecting his teaching to private judgement:

If you had lived in the time of the Apostles, your first question would have been, Do they come from God? and you would have determined this by private judgment—but, when you once believed, if they said to you 'The dead will one day rise,' you would not have said 'I am not so sure of that, I have not yet proved it'—or if you had, they would have answered, 'But we tell you they will—you have come to be *taught*—If you want to find it out for yourselves, do so—but then you should not come to *us*.'[5]

To return to a matter touched on earlier in this chapter: it is now obvious that no rejection by Newman of the notion of 'absolute obedience' implies that the antithesis between going by the authority of the Church and going by private judgement is illusory. The illusion was to be exposed by the fact that the partisans on each side have to appeal in the last resort to private judgement (or 'conscience'). But two different uses of private judgement distinguished by Newman were confused. The private judgement to which both partisans have to appeal is on the claim of an institution that its teaching comes from divine revelation, a claim the acceptance of which renders inconsistent the use of private judgement to determine what has been revealed.

[5] Newman to an unknown correspondent, 27 Nov. 1874; *Letters and Diaries*, xxvii. 162.

There would be some intertwining of the credibility of what is taught as divinely revealed and the credentials of its teacher, in a complete statement of Newman's opinion. The holiness of someone claiming to teach in God's name is judged by those addressed, and this judgement will not be cut off from judgement on the moral character of the teaching. Beyond that, there is 'an inward witness to the truth of the Gospel. In the sermon which has these words as its title this witness follows upon lived-out belief—'You may, if you will, have an inward witness arising from obedience.'[6] In 'The Nature of Faith in Relation to Reason' (one of the *University Sermons*, its date 1839) the teaching elicits an *antecedent* testimony to itself, given that the heart in those to whom comes is right; and to an exent it authenticates the teacher:

The Word of Life is offered to a man; and on its being offered, he has Faith in it. Why? On these two grounds,—the word of its human messenger, and the likelihood of the message . . . to what it seems to him Divine Goodness would vouchsafe did He vouchsafe any . . . (pp. 202–3)

Though there can be seen to be the intertwining of an intrinsic credibility in what is taught with the credentials of the teacher, when the things Newman says in different places are brought together, the emphasis is heavily upon the credentials of the teacher. Thought of the content of revelation as drawing belief towards itself is altogether absent from a passage in the *Grammar of Assent* stressing the kind of revelation the Christian one is. God might have

imparted to us truths which nature cannot teach us, without telling us that He had imparted them . . . But the very idea of Chrisianity in its profession and history, is something more than this . . . it is a definite message from God to man distinctly conveyed by His chosen instruments, and to be received as such a message . . . and maintained as true, on the ground of its being divine, not as true on intrinsic grounds . . .

In consequence, the exhibition of credentials, that is, of evidence, that it is what it professes to be, is essential to Christianity, as it comes to us; for we are not left at liberty to pick and choose out of its contents according to our judgment but must receive it all, as we find

---

[6] *Parochial and Plain Sermons*, viii. 122. These sermons were preached between 1828 and 1843.

it, if we accept it at all. (*Grammar of Assent*, ch. 10, introduction, pp. 386–7)

The question how we are to ascertain the content of revelation is given its Catholic answer in this passage, and this answer its rationale: we are taught by the Church what has been revealed, in a revelation the nature of which excludes our deciding for ourselves upon its content. Whether or not revelation is to be found in Scripture alone, as Protestantism maintains, divides Protestantism from Catholicism less significantly than their disagreement over the way in which the content of revelation is to be ascertained from Scripture. In the Protestant view it is by private judgement.

Newman had observed as an Anglican that the policy of deciding for oneself from Scripture on the essentials of Christian belief was liable to reach the conclusion 'that there are no essentials at all'.[7] One of two later arguments, very individually his own, against the notion of determining by private judgement what has been divinely revealed is the following:

No system of opinions, ever given to the world, approved itself in all its parts to the reason of any one individual by whom it was mastered. No revelation then is conceivable, which does not involve, almost in its very idea as being something new, a collision with the human intellect, and demands accordingly, if it is to be accepted, a sacrifice of private judgment on the part of those to whom it is addressed. If a revelation be necessary, then also in consequence is that sacrifice necessary. One man will have to make a sacrifice in one respect, another in another, all men in some.[8]

(Newman did not of course think, as this passage by itself might suggest, that revelation consists in the divine communication of a number of propositions; he did think that its having a propositional aspect was absolutely essential to the notion of a revelation. Deprived of its propositional aspect Christianity dissolved into objectless sentiment.) The contention in the other argument is that the policy of deciding for oneself from Scripture what has been revealed is inconsistent with

[7] *Prophetical Office of the Church*, lect. 9, § 2, p. 215.
[8] 'An Internal Argument for Christianity' (1866), in *Discussions and Arguments*, p. 397.

faith, the correlative of revelation, inconsistent with faith as the Apostles understood it. The faith the Apostles required— faith in their word 'as being God's word'—requires obedience. Are not

these two states or acts of mind quite distinct from each other;—to believe simply what a living authority tells you, and to take a book, such as Scripture, and to use it as you please, to master it, that is, to make yourself the master of it, to interpret it for yourself . . . Are not these two procedures distinct in this, that in the former you submit, in the latter you judge?[9]

The boundary between what the Church has determined to be revealed truth and what is left open to private judgement may well be indefinite. To many doctrines the commitment of the Church may be so manifest that to question whether they are part of its teaching would be tantamount to questioning its teaching; there may well be others whose status is ambiguous. How strongly Newman resisted encroachment on the legitimate domain of private judgement can be seen from his attitude to the movement to have papal infallibility defined as dogma by the Vatican Council. The prospect was 'thunder in the clear sky'. 'No impending danger is to be averted, but a great difficulty is to be created.'[10] Newman was not anticipating a difficulty in belief for himself; papal infallibility was an *opinion* his private judgement went along with. This opinion 'an aggressive insolent faction' aimed at forcing on everyone in the Church by having it transformed into an article of faith. In the event, the actual definition of the doctrine came as a relief to him. Extreme infallibilist pretension (including that of Pius IX himself, Newman thought[11]) had been 'overruled'. As circumscribed by the dogma, papal infallibility would have (and would have had) a rare exercise. While Newman said that if the Council were to make papal infallibility a dogma he would 'with every Catholic' accept this decision,[12] in the event

---

[9] 'Faith and Private Judgment' (1849), *Discourses to Mixed Congregations*, p. 199. These are Catholic sermons. The 'obedience of faith' is, however, every bit as strongly emphasized in one of the Anglican *University Sermons*, 'Wilfulness, the Sin of Saul' (1832). Missing from the Anglican sermon, naturally, is the notion in the Catholic sermon of obedience to a living, contemporary authority in matters of faith.

[10] Newman to Bishop Ullathorne, 28 Jan. 1870; *Letters and Diaries*, xxv. 18–19.

[11] Newman to Miss Holmes, 15 May 1871; ibid. 330.

[12] Newman to Bishop Brown, 8 Apr. 1870; ibid. 83.

it was not his opinion that the Council's decision altogether settled the question. In the Letter to the Duke of Norfolk (§ 8, pp. 301–3) he quotes from a letter he had written just after the dogma was decided upon, which raises several questions as to the validity of its decree. One of these questions has to do with the 'moral unanimity' of the Council. It is raised in private judgement on a council properly summoned and larger than any previous council, as Newman notes; and the conditions for answering it he himself decides upon. Emphasized is the future judgement of the whole Church on the definition[13]—a judgement, it is to be observed, like private judgement as not delivered in any formal procedure, unlike it in not being that of an individual.

An indeterminacy in the boundary between the domains of doctrinal authority and private judgement, the existence of territory in which both have legitimate interests, is presupposed in the following passage, unusually dramatic and obscure, from the *Apologia*:

It is the custom with Protestant writers to consider that, whereas there are two great principles in action in the history of religion, Authority and Private Judgment, they have all the Private Judgment to themselves, and we have the full inheritance and the super-incumbent oppression of Authority. But this is not so; it is the vast Catholic body itself, and it only, which affords an arena for both combatants . . . It is necessary for the very life of religion, viewed in its large operations and its history, that the warfare should be incessantly carried on. Every exercise of Infallibility is brought into act by an intense and varied operation of the Reason, both as its ally and as its opponent, and provokes again, when it has done its work, a re-action of Reason against it; and, as in a civil polity the State exists and endures by means of the rivalry and collision, the encroachments and defeats of its constituent parts, so in like manner

---

[13] 'And further, if the definition is consistently received by the whole body of the faithful, as valid, or as the expression of a truth, then too it will claim our assent by force of the great dictum, "Securus judicat orbis terrarum".' (A translation of the dictum given by Newman on one occasion when he cites it in this context is 'The judgment of the whole Church has no chance of being wrong': Newman to Mrs Wilson, 24 Oct. 1870; *Letters and Diaries*, xxv. 220.) A comment in the Postscript to the Letter to the Duke of Norfolk (pp. 371–2) shows Newman's anxiety not to be thought of as holding that 'subsequent reception by the Church' enters into the notion of a validly defined article of faith. At issue over the definition of papal infallibility were the credentials of a particular council.

Catholic Christendom is no simple exhibition of religious absolutism, but presents a continuous picture of Authority, and Private Judgment alternatively advancing and retreating . . . (ch. 5, p. 252)

When Newman speaks of the two principles as being active in the 'history of religion', he is not making an observation from the perspective of comparative religion; he is referring only to the Christian religion viewed as divided into Catholicism and Protestantism. When further down the passage he speaks of the necessity of both principles to 'the life of religion', the Catholic religion is clearly meant.

Why are both principles necessary to the life of the Catholic religion? As Newman saw it, the principle of authority is necessary for the reasons indicated earlier in this section: briefly, because the Christian revelation 'is not given, if there be no authority to decide what it is that is given'.[14] The principle of private judgement is necessary if the credentials of a claimant to authority in the matter of revelation are to be investigated. But in the passage before us, private judgement is not engaged in any such investigation; its engagement is in some way with doctrine itself—in an exploration of its content. Why should this be thought *necessary* to the life of religion? An answer is that the development of doctrine is necessary to the life of religion, and the operation of private judgement on doctrine necessary to this development.

Viewed in one way, Christianity 'came into the world as an idea'. That time and thought 'are necessary for the full comprehension or perfection of great ideas' is a foundational theme of the *Essay on the Development of Doctrine*.[15] It is theologians who think investigatively about doctrine, not those whose office in the Church is its preservation. The theologian's thinking freely about a doctrine, though not calling it in question, can in fact be endangering it; and on the other hand, the bearers of the Church's authority can see it as endangered when in fact it is not: hence the 'warfare'. Since Newman speaks of the intervention of infallibility, the warfare must be directly over doctrine; theological speculation generating the appearance of heresy or, the reality of it,

---

[14] *Essay on Development*, ch. 2, § 2, p. 89.
[15] Ibid., ch. 1 ('On the Development of Ideas'). The quotations are from ch. 2, § 2 (p. 77) and from the introduction (p. 29).

countered by authority guarding the doctrine, acting in its various ways. (The theme of this passage is partially resumed some pages further on in the *Apologia*, where it becomes clear what Newman had in mind when he said that infallibility is brought into act by the operation of Reason as ally and opponent—the councils of the Church, in the condemnation of heresy, have availed themselves of argument against argument. And a teleological aspect of the warfare makes an appearance in the later passage, in the contribution of 'heretical questionings' to the construction of the dogmas Newman found so satisfying, intellectually and religiously.)

Not referred to in the passage we have been considering is the conflict between authority and private judgement which is indirectly over doctrine, over what is related to it, to use an image of Newman's, as a country's territorial waters are to its territory. Recognizing it as a 'great trial to the Reason', Newman defends the Church's right to issue injunctions on matters which merely have a bearing on matters of faith. ('It could not act in its own province, unless it had the right to act out of it.') Belief is not imposed as regards these matters, Newman points out, silence might be—the profession of a certain opinion, for instance, disallowed; what is asked for is external compliance. Even though these injunctions may later be tacitly withdrawn, they are to be obeyed.[16] In comment upon them Newman mentions the past history of the Church, but the outstanding time of encroachment on private judge-

---

[16] *Apologia*, ch. 5, p. 257. Newman's 'most intimate thought' on ecclesiastical control over the expression of opinion on matters which merely bear upon matters of faith is not to be found in the *Apologia*, Edmond Cormier maintains; 'under a cloud at Rome', he had to be very careful about what he said in public (*La Liberté de conscience et de pensée selon J. H. Newman* (Montreal, 1964), 45). A letter of Newman's to Robert Ornsby (26 Mar. 1863; *Letters and Diaries*, xx. 426), written shortly before the publication of the *Apologia*, is drawn upon in particular by Cormier. Part of the background to the letter is a communication from Pius IX to the Archbishop of Munich asserting, on the occasion of a meeting of Catholic scholars at Munich, the deference due by Catholics to ecclesiastical authority even in secular enquiry. The letter to Ornsby, a private analysis of the Munich Brief made by Newman, and the draft of a letter to Acton commenting on the Brief, are to be found in Wilfrid Ward's *Life of Cardinal Newman* (London, 1912), i. 565–6, 641–2; ii. 49–50. There is nothing in this material inconsistent with any statement in the *Apologia*, but it reveals great dislike of anything approaching a policy of ecclesiastical interference in matters adjacent to matters of faith, and great apprehension as to its consequences.

ment by inquisitorial authority was the mid-nineteenth century; and a notable example of its spirit was the delation to Rome, three of four years before the publication of the *Apologia*, of Newman's article 'On Consulting the Faithful in Matters of Doctrine'.

III

I must begin with the Creator and His creature, when I would draw out the prerogatives and the supreme authority of Conscience. (Letter to the Duke of Norfolk, § 5, p. 246)

With these words Newman begins the substantiation of his claim that the dictate of conscience will overrule 'the word of a pope'.

In the Letter to the Duke of Norfolk conscience is viewed as having what might be called primordial authority. Conscience goes back to creation. It has the antecedence of natural religion, of which it is the principle, to revealed religion, which is in part a 'republication' of natural religion.[17] It is foundational to the mission of the Church, and of the papacy. We need to see whether any inferences can be drawn from the actual descriptions of this threefold priority of conscience to everything ecclesiastical which would support the claim being made for an overriding authority in conscience. None are in fact drawn by Newman. Consideration of this question will bring into view nearly everything with a bearing on his remark that in a toast he would drink to conscience first and then to the pope. It comes right at the end of the section of the Letter which has conscience as its express topic, and which begins by linking conscience with creation. It follows a citation of theological opinion to the effect that conscience is always to be obeyed. The title of conscience to obedience in all circumstances completes what needs to be assembled for an understanding of the remark.

[17] Discussing in one place in the *Grammar of Assent* the anticipations of revealed religion in natural religion, Newman pauses at a certain counter intimation emanating fron conscience. Its forcing us to realize our unshiftable responsibility for our actions, and its forebodings, go against the notion of vicarious reparation involved in the doctrine of the atonement (ch. 10, § 1, p. 394).

We consider first whether conscience has the authority
Newman claimed for it in virture of its being the principle of
natural religion. It is immediately apparent that it does not.
Conscience, 'the sense of right and wrong', is at once 'the
highest of all teachers, yet the least luminous' (in the
Grammar of Assent Newman spoke of the 'twilight of natural
religion'); 'so easily puzzled, obscured, perverted . . . so
impressible by education, so biassed by pride and passion, so
unsteady' as to be in great need of what revealed religion
supplies and it is part of the pope's mission to declare (Letter,
pp. 253–4).[18]

It is not to be thought that the view expressed here is
inconsistent with any overruling of the pope's authority by
conscience. Asserting that conscience can overrule 'the word
of a pope', Newman has in mind the pope's jurisdictional
office, and particular injunctions he might issue; here the
reference is to the pope's teaching office, and general moral
and religious truths. We might well, however, be feeling
uneasiness about Newman's consistency on another ground.
How is he going to be able to ascribe to conscience an
authority which is supreme, when he subordinates its deliverances in the moral field to the teaching of the Church, by
having them liable to rectification by this teaching? It is much
too early to deal with the question, but it may be usefully
remarked now that to say simply, as is so often done, that for
Newman conscience is supreme is to say about the most
obfuscating thing that could be said of his views on conscience.

Conscience certainly derives no title to any overriding of
papal authority in virtue of its being a rectifiable sense of
right and wrong, though one that has been primordially in
existence. But in the *Grammar of Assent* it was not conscience

---

[18] The following sentences, from a work written twenty-five years earlier, by
themselves would falsely suggest something much more sweeping: 'Revelation
consists in . . . the substitution of the voice of a Lawgiver for the voice of conscience.
The supremacy of conscience is the essence of natural religion; the supremacy of
Apostle, or Pope, or Church . . . is the essence of revealed' (*Essay on Development*
(1845), ch. 2, § 2, p. 86). Ecclesiastical authority where once conscience held sway!
That would both miss Newman's point and distort its implication. As the context
shows, he is contrasting natural religion, as having in conscience a 'subjective
authority', with revealed religion, which makes available an 'objective' one. And a few
lines down the page he asserts of conscience what he always does, that it is 'ever to be
obeyed'.

as a sense of right and wrong that was 'the creative principle of religion'; it was conscience as a magisterial dictate. Of course, for Newman conscience is both the one and the other. And to anticipate the conclusion we shall reach, it is in virtue of its magisterial character that the dictate of conscience can overrule the word of a pope; the priority of natural to revealed religion is an irrelevant consideration. So also, as we shall see, is the presupposition of conscience by the pope's mission.

Conscience, in an elaborate figure, is depicted by Newman as exercising prior to the institution of the papacy an office analogous to that of the pope, an office—so the context implies—which it still retains:

> Conscience . . . is a messenger from Him, who, both in nature and in grace, speaks to us behind a veil, and teaches and rules us by his representatives. Conscience is the aboriginal Vicar of Christ, a prophet in its informations, a monarch in its peremptoriness, a priest in its blessings and anathemas, and, even though the eternal priesthood throughout the Church could cease to be, in it the sacerdotal principle would remain and would have a sway . . . (Letter, § 5, pp. 248–9)

Newman is not concerned in this passage with conscience as foundational to the pope's mission. But this juxtaposition of the pope with his primordial predecessor and his contemporary is a very important part of the setting of the claim that conscience has an authority far higher than that of any papal injunction. And this is as good an occasion as we shall have to notice something contained in the passage which is additional to everything else that Newman says of conscience.

It will have been observed that from this constellation of titles one is picked out and spoken of in a way clearly implying it to be more than metaphorical: in conscience the sacerdotal principle is instantiated. Made at a time when priesthood and conscience were liable to seem even opposed in notion, the claim is paradoxical in itself. It has been seen as theologically important. What foundation does it have in Newman's own ontology of conscience? No foundation. And the objection might continue: A priest mediates a relationship with divinity. Conceiving of conscience non-entitatively, Newman does not give it the differentiation from its possessor necessary for it to be a mediator. Conscience is no more other than oneself than one's intelligence is. To this the reply can be made that in Newman's phenomenology of conscience it has all the otherness required for the analogy: a priest differentiated by his office from himself can offer sacrifice for himself as well as for others. It is then objected that this reply itself makes visible the respect in which the analogy does break down. A priest offers sacrifice; and there is nothing comparable to this action in the actions ascribed to conscience in Newman's conception of it, according to which what conscience does is to determine right and wrong, and to command, prohibit, accuse, acquit, condemn, and bestow benison. This objection could be countered by some remark to the effect that the last two actions are all that is claimed and needed for there to be a priestly mediation through conscience. But the objector was right in fastening on the need for something as central to priesthood as the offering of sacrifice. If all that conscience relevantly does is analogous to the delivering of benedictions and its opposite, the claim that conscience instantiates the sacerdotal principle loses both paradoxicality and point.

Several things call for attention in the account Newman gives of conscience as foundational to the pope's mission. 'On the law of conscience and its sacredness are founded both his authority in theory', Newman writes, 'and his power in fact' (Letter, p. 252). This is a surprising foundation for the pope's authority in *theory*. It is explained up to a point by Newman's having said just previously that it is the pope's 'very mission to proclaim the moral law'. Amplified, the explanation is that according to the theology of revelation which Newman had in mind, the moral law, knowable by 'the light of nature' (by 'conscience', to use his alternative term) known, as things are, only fitfully in this manner, is definitively made known by revelation, from which also the pope derives his teaching office. The explanation is incomplete because this is a paradoxical limiting of the pope's mission, needing the comment, indeed more than the comment, later supplied by Newman: 'In saying all this, of course I must not be supposed to be limiting the Revelation of which the Church is the keeper to a mere republication of the Natural Law' (p. 254). (Nothing of theoretical, let alone doctrinal, substance is claimed for conscience in the Letter to the Duke of Norfolk which Newman would have disallowed elsewhere. The distortion of emphasis being noticed here results probably from a sense of the need, in meeting the charge that conscience was an abject thing in the Catholic Church, to give it great prominence.)

Newman goes on to say that while revelation transcends the teaching of nature, it is not independent of it but is its 'complement . . . embodiment, and interpretation'. This is followed by a remark which, encountered in isolation, could be misunderstood: 'The Pope, who comes of Revelation, has no jurisdiction over Nature.' The misunderstanding (blocked by the view that the pope's mission is to proclaim the moral law and, immediately, by Newman's bringing the 'interpretation' of Nature within the sphere of Revelation) would be to suppose him to be maintaining that it would be usurpatory for the pope (and, more generally, the Church) to attempt to lay down what was morally right and wrong; since here Nature is the teacher. What exactly Newman did mean by the remark would be conjectural. Nothing that follows it elucidates it. To have been expected was something indicating how what the pope could teach in the moral field was circumscribed. What actually follows the remark is to the effect that if the pope failed to preach the virtues and, even more, if he 'trampled on the conscience' of his people, his rule would not last.

By giving such prominence to the moral law and natural religion in this account of revelation and the pope's mission, Newman brings conscience into corresponding prominence. But the effect is to make an important and already cryptic assertion—the assertion which leads in to what we have just now been looking at—harder to understand. Anxious to drive it home that the pope could not 'speak against conscience', Newman asserts (p. 252) that the Church itself is 'built' on 'the right and duty of following that Divine Authority, the voice of conscience'. How the Church is built on conscience is not explained. But both the Church and the papacy within it would be built upon conscience in the same way, and the following explanation is given of a dependency of the pope on conscience:

it is by the univeral sense of right and wrong, the consciousness of transgression, the pangs of guilt, and the dread of retribution, as first principles, deeply lodged in the hearts of men, it is thus and only thus, that he has gained his footing in the world and achieved his success. It is his claim to come from the Divine Lawgiver, in order to elicit, protect, and enforce those truths which the Lawgiver has sown in our very nature, it is this and this only, that is the explanation of his length of life . . . The championship of the Moral Law and of conscience is his *raison d'être*. (p. 253)

It could be only on the rarest of occasions that Newman is substantially mistaken about human motivation, especially where religion is involved. He is so here. The pope does not owe his power to his being seen as upholding the moral law to which our consciences bear witness: in so far as he can be said to owe his power to any single thing it is to the belief that he holds 'the keys of the kingdom of heaven'. Near the beginning of the passage, however, are to be found the elements of another explanation of the way in which the pope's rule has a foundation in conscience, one which would explain his power. Given the belief that the pope rules by divine authority, conscience, with the pangs of guilt and dread of retribution in reserve, will require that he be obeyed. But we were looking for some dependency of pope on conscience which might justify an overriding of the pope by conscience. Obviously, we have not found it in this explanation of the way in which his rule is based on conscience.

Still looking for this justification, we have finally to consider any prerogatives conscience might derive from its being coeval with our creation. As he had begun with Scripture, and the early Church, when he spoke of the pope's prerogatives, so, Newman says, 'I must begin with the Creator and His creature, when I would draw out the prerogatives and the supreme authority of Conscience' (Letter, p. 246). There is an implicit contrast here between the authority of conscience as belonging to the order of creation, and the authority of the pope as belonging to the order of salvation, but no inference is drawn from it. The point to which Newman proceeds is that creating us, God implants in our intelligence the eternal moral law;[19] this law, 'as apprehended in the minds of individual

---

[19] Newman is not enunciating here a view incompatible with one holding that knowledge of the moral law is obtained by some sort of reasoning from the awareness of particular moral truths; he is saying a traditional thing which could easily be brought into harmony with any view in the epistemology of morals plausibly attributable to him.

men', he says, is conscience. The connecting of an autonomous apprehension of the moral law with our creation does not suggest any overriding of the authority of the pope by that of conscience. And when Newman straightaway says that this law 'may suffer refraction in passing into the intellectual medium' of each person apprehending it (p. 247), what is suggested is, rather, the overriding of conscience by the pope; for this remark indicates the need which, according to Newman's theological beliefs, was met by revelation, and the authority instituted by it with the power to rectify conscience. What is it, then, that in the present context leads Newman to speak of 'the supreme authority of Conscience'? Only this: whatever refraction the moral law suffers in anyone's conscience, 'it is not therefore so affected as to lose its character of being the Divine Law, but still has, as such, the prerogative of commanding obedience' (p. 247). Mistaken or not, the dictate of conscience presents itself as the dictate of the supreme Law-giver.

The theme centring on the primordial character of the authority of conscience can now be brought to an end. It is not because conscience goes back to our creation, has the priority of natural to revealed religion, is foundational to the mission of the Church and the papacy; it is not in virtue of any of these considerations, or of all of them together, that Newman maintains the authority of conscience to be supreme. On what, then, does he ground this supremacy? Its ground, not explicitly asserted in the Letter to the Duke of Norfolk but fragmentarily disclosed when the right of conscience to command obedience is linked with 'the Divine Law' and with the sense of conscience as 'a divine voice', is the imperative of conscience as this is described in the *Grammar of Assent*. Newman's reason for asserting of conscience supreme authority is the uniquely magisterial quality of its dictates. What can appear to be other reasons he is giving for this assertion turn out to be only a setting for it.

What light is thrown by what we have been looking at on the precedence of conscience over the pope, in the after-dinner toast? This precedence reflects, it is to be supposed, that of the primordial over what comes later in time. But the primordiality of conscience is not taken by Newman to bestow a title upon conscience to override papal authority in any matter. It is, however, further to be supposed that Newman's remark reflects his contention that we have a duty to obey conscience in all circumstances, even when these might be such that obedience to conscience involves disobedience to the pope. What this duty of obedience to conscience amounts to remains to be determined, but of more immediate consequence for an understanding of the remark is that it is made in reference to the pope's jurisdictional authority. For reasons we shall come to, Newman thought that collision between conscience and the pope over matters of belief was impossible, so the precedence accorded to conscience reflects no precedence in such a collision. We easily imagine that we understand this endlessly quoted remark. The fact is that we are not in a position to know what to make of it until its occurrence is looked at in § 5 of the Letter to the Duke of Norfolk, and even then some doubt remains. In part an expression of the principle that conscience is always to be obeyed, it expresses no principle specifically governing the relation between conscience and the Church. And it sums nothing up.

Conscience has to be distinguished from a 'counterfeit'. It could be a very troublesome distinction to make; Newman's purposes enable it to be made easily enough. These are to show the character conscience must possess if a person is ever to go by his conscience against what the pope enjoins, and to show that the 'liberty of conscience' condemned by two popes in the nineteenth century is properly called 'so-called liberty of conscience'. (Newman's discussion of this second matter will be noticed in a later chapter.) Conscience, as seen by Newman, is the direct creation of God, 'a principle planted within us, before we have had any training'. As recreated by nineteenth-century ideas, it is 'a twist in primitive and untutored man', its dictate, in one way or another, disqualified from being taken to voice what God requires (Letter, p. 249). That is the background to the distinction between conscience and its counterfeit. The distinction itself is that the one imposes an obligation regarded as coming from God—or, at any rate, as altogether ungainsayable; the other expresses 'self will'. (Easily made, it is not, of course, a distinction always easily applied.) Newman would have rejected the criticism

that he had not described a plausible counterfeit of conscience:
he did not think that the name of conscience was plausibly
invoked in contemporary demands for various rights.

IV

If conscience has 'supreme authority', if it must never be
disobeyed, it will override more than some particular command,
some jurisdictional injunction of a pope, you would suppose.
Is there any exercise of ecclesiastical authority which it could
not override? None at all, as Bremond reads Newman:

> If I allow the primacy of conscience, if I submit to other authorities
> only when conscience itself shows me that this submission is due, it
> will come about logically, that before I assent to some 'defined
> doctrine', I will examine it, appraise it from the point of view of
> conscience; ready to believe or to refuse belief according as this
> doctrine seems to me fitted to enrich my moral life, to give it
> precision, to support it, to complete the inspirations of my
> conscience . . .
>
> You have made my conscience the supreme judge from whose
> verdict there is no appeal; you have no more right to limit its
> competence than to cancel its dictates.[20]

In an appraisal of this confrontation of Newman with what
are seen as the implications of his own teaching on conscience,
it is essential to take into account the perspective from which it
is marshalled: that of someone within the Church or that of
someone outside it. But first there is an objection to be raised
on Newman's behalf in either case. To pronounce judgement

[20] H. Bremond, *Newman: Essai de biographie psychologique*, epilogue, pp. 344–5.
A psychological contention of Bremond's is that the 'antinomy' between the claims of
conscience and the claims of Christian doctrine is resolved in Newman's own life. And
implicity making the distinction, habitual with Newman, between seeing some matter
abstractly and in concrete reality, Bremond allows that, like Newman, 'believers will
not hesitate to drink "to conscience first, and to the Pope afterwards", certain as they
are that in concrete reality, the infallible representative of God will always be the
spokesman of conscience.' A psychological remark near the end of Bremond's book
replaces, in effect, the assertion (quoted earlier in this essay) that the whole of
Newman's theology is directed towards showing the identity of the God of conscience
with the God of revelation. Newman, it is merely said, by 'une association invincible'
regarded the dictates of his conscience as expressions of the will of the God of
Christian dogma (pp. 328–9).

upon a doctrine is beyond the competence of the conscience to which Newman ascribed supreme authority: its dictates bear 'immediately upon conduct', are 'practical' dictates (Letter to the Duke of Norfolk, § 5, p. 256.) And the reason why only as issuing such a dictate (or, in Newman's alternative way of speaking, only as being such a dictate) does conscience have 'supremacy', 'supreme authority', would be that only then does it have a magisterial character that cannot be gainsaid. These terms apply to the overawing conscience around which cluster the phenomena described in the *Grammar of Assent.* Conscience, in the passage quoted from Bremond, scrutinizing a doctrine to see whether among other things it is fitted to promote the enrichment of one's moral life, recalls the Shaftesburian type of conscience criticized by Newman in *The Idea of a University*—conscience reduced to a mere moral sense merging into mere moral taste.

We now consider the significance of the perspective from which Newman is confronted by Bremond's speaker. If it is that of someone outside the Church, an enquirer, then Newman's objection, apart from the point that has just been raised, would be to the attempt to assess doctrines, put forward as revealed truth, by their content, the proper object of enquiry being into the credentials of their teacher.

For Bremond Newman's conversion to Catholicism would be falsely exteriorized if it is thought to conform to the opinions that conscience does not pronounce upon doctrine, and that enquiry into a claim to teach revealed truth is properly directed towards the credentials of the teacher. The part played by conscience in Newman's conversion should not go altogether without remark in this essay. It is touched on in a brief digression here.

Bremond saw Newman's conversion as a paradoxical work of conscience.[21] 'There is nothing more individual . . . than conscience.' Newman, ruled by his conscience, Newman, for whom there were two and only two self-evidently existent beings, himself and his Creator,[22] might 'logically' have been expected to look for 'no other Church than himself'. But he was born into a Church, and his conscience endorsed the

[21] Ibid., epilogue, pp. 331 ff.
[22] See *Apologia pro Vita Sua*, ch. 1, p. 4.

existence of the Church and Christian dogma. And when the Church of his birth was seeming to him to fail, his thoughts turned to one 'better able to respond to the desires and needs of his conscience'. 'The needs of his conscience led him to Rome.' The *Apologia pro Vita Sua*, in fact, tells a story altogether other than anything like this could suggest. Nothing that happens in it impelling Newman towards Rome was a need of his conscience making itself felt, or a perception of his conscience. To bear this out, it is sufficient to mention the shock which began the process of his conversion and the reflection it led on to—'The thought for the moment had been "The Church of Rome will be found right after all" '—and the 'three blows' which broke him near the end.[23] But did he not himself attribute his conversion to his having followed his conscience? 'A faulty conscience faithfully obeyed, through God's mercy, had in the long run brought me right.'[24] He did not mean that his conscience dictated his *thought*. It required him to *do*, as doing the will of God, what the situation in which he found himself called for. He looked to his reason to settle upon that. 'The one question was, [in consequence of 'the dreadful misgiving'], what was I to do? I had to make up my mind for myself . . . I determined to be guided, not by my imagination, but by my reason.'[25]

We return to the confrontation of Newman with what Bremond takes to be implied by his teaching on conscience, this time supposing the point of view from which Newman is addressed to be that of someone inside the Church. The primacy of conscience 'logically' requires him, he tells Newman, to approach a doctrine, belief withheld, until he

---

[23] Ibid., ch. 3, p. 118, 139 ff.

[24] Letter to Pusey, § 1, in *Difficulties of Anglicans*, ii. 6.

[25] *Apologia*, ch. 3, p. 119. In keeping with the role of conscience in his own case, Newman writes, 'there are those . . . who would be Catholics if their conscience would let them . . . but they cannot, as a matter of duty, enter its fold on account of certain great difficulties which block their way . . . when they would embrace that faith which look so like what it professes to be' (Preface to 3rd edn. *Prophetical Office of the Church*, in *The Via Media*, vol. i, p. xxxvi). An example of the sort of difficulties Newman had in mind is the one which his theory of the development of doctrine was aimed at meeting, the appearance of innovations by the Catholic Church on an unchangeable Apostolic teaching. Labouring the point, they are difficulties which it would be impossible for conscience, however enlarged in notion, to come up with or weigh up. Conscience is brought in by Newman in connection with the action of someone faced with them.

sees whether or not it recommends itself to his conscience. Newman would see him as in an impossible position, both religiously and logically. Religiously, because—to use a phrase which for Newman expressed the attitude due in a person professing adherence to a religion he acknowledges to be revealed—the 'obedience of faith' is refused. Logically, because of the incoherence in acknowledging the claims of the Church and querying some part of the teaching to which it has committed itself.

This would answer Bremond inadequately. If the believer's conscience has to give way before the teaching authority of the Church, the claims Newman makes for conscience should have been abated: the confrontation of Newman supposedly with himself could have taken this direction. In fact, it will turn out that no claims need to be abated, neither those made for conscience, nor those of the Church. For the rest of the chapter we shall be occupied with various matters leading up to this conclusion.

V

It is an unfortunate consequence of the polemical circumstances in which the Letter to the Duke of Norfolk was composed that Newman's interest is not primarily, is hardly at all, in the relation between conscience and the teaching office of the Church. That, as having separate domains, they are not competing authorities is the implication of an argument cast in the form of one or two remarks, which is a step in another argument he was conducting. But their relationship was not an issue. And over parts of what is to be found in the Letter bearing on their relationship hangs an obscurity which would have been removed if Newman had had this topic significantly in mind. His concern was with an objection to the possibility of any genuine freedom of conscience in the Catholic system. He met this objection with an argument to show that if conscience and the pope, operating in the same domain (as they can do when the pope 'legislates, or gives particular orders, and the like'), were to clash, conscience would have the final say.

Abstractly stated, the objection might seem too extravagant to deserve the trouble of the answer Newman gives to it, but it was a reality to many in the audience to which the Letter was addressed. Expressing an anticipated reaction to what he had maintained of conscience as related to the pope's mission, he writes:

It may be said that no one doubts that the Pope's power rests on those weaknesses of human nature, that religious sense, which in ancient days Lucretius noted as the cause of the worst ills of our race; that he uses it dexterously . . . and that thus conscience becomes his creature . . . doing, as if on a divine sanction his will; so that . . . in idea it is free, but never free in fact . . . (Letter, § 5, p. 255)

Newman's reply to the objection does not confine itself to reaching the small conclusion that the Catholic system provides for a genuine independence of conscience. It argues for the claim that conscience can overrule *any* papal injunction.

Far more interesting than even the strong conclusion of this reply, however, is the question whether Newman's separation of their domains prevents a collision between conscience and the teaching office of the Church. The claim that conscience can overrule any papal injunction was not one which Newman innovatively made. If the Letter to the Duke of Norfolk was to fulfil its purpose, it had to be seen as one which could be backed up by authoritative Catholic opinion. And so when the reasoning is over, citations are made from 'recognized authors'. If the claim is allowed, and if Newman's separation of their domains prevents a collision between conscience and the teaching office of the Church, the result will be that nowhere does conscience have to yield to the authority of the Church.

Our primary concern, then, is with an argument which Newman had no occasion to elaborate, and which has to be disengaged from the course of reasoning which it was designed to fit. We need to have this course of reasoning fully before us, but its stages—in Newman's numbering—will be summarized when his actual words are not important. We need first his statement of the objection to the possibility of an independent Catholic conscience, to which it is a reply. The objection is that if conscience was 'able to exert a will of its own',

> there would ensue a collision more unmanageable than that between the Church and the State, as being in one and the same subject-matter—viz., religion; for what would become of the Pope's 'absolute authority,' as Mr. Gladstone calls it, if the private conscience had an absolute authority also? (Letter, § 5, p. 255)

Newman's reply is as follows:

1. By 'conscience' is to be understood, not 'an opinion', but what is taken to be 'a divine voice, speaking within us'.

2. Conscience

> is not a judgment upon any speculative truth, any abstract doctrine, but bears immediately on conduct, on something to be done or not done. 'Conscience,' says St. Thomas, 'is the practical judgment or dictate of reason, by which we judge what *hic et nunc* is to be done as being good, or to be avoided as evil.' Hence conscience cannot come into direct collision with the Church's or the Pope's infallibility; which is engaged on general propositions, and in the condemnation of particular and given errors. (p. 256)

3. Conscience

> being a practical dictate, a collision is possible between it and the Pope's authority only when the Pope legislates, or gives particular orders, and the like. But a Pope is not infallible in his laws, nor in his commands, nor in his acts of state, nor in his administration, nor in his public policy . . . Since then infallibility alone could block the exercise of conscience, and the Pope is not infallible in that subject-matter in which conscience is of supreme authority, no dead-lock, such as is implied in the objection which I am answering, can take place between conscience and the Pope. (pp. 256–7)

4. When conscience 'has the right of opposing the supreme, though not infallible Authority of the Pope', its dictate, 'in order to prevail against the voice of the Pope, must follow upon . . . prayer, and all available means of arriving at a right judgment on the matter in question' (pp. 257–8).

How, in summary, has the objection to the possibility of an independent Catholic conscience been answered? The objection was that an encounter between conscience and papal authority, being in the same 'subject-matter'—'religion'—would be deadlocked. Why would there be this deadlock? The reason has to be inferred from the way the objection is answered, and it seems to be this: conscience and infallibility would each encounter in the other an insurmountable obstacle to its exercise. And the objection is answered by an argument to the effect that the encounter is impossible because infallibility and conscience do not have the same subject-matter. The objection answered, Newman goes on to reach his strong conclusion: where there is a coincidence of subject-matter or of 'domain' (to change to his easier word) as between the authority of conscience and that of the pope, infallibility—the only match for conscience—is absent, and conscience 'prevails'.

The question now is what the domains are in which the pope and conscience operate, and how they are assigned. Two domains of authority are assigned to the pope; in one he is endowed with infallibility, in the other he is not. 'The Pope's infallibility . . . lies in matters speculative, and his prerogative of authority is no infallibility in laws, commands, or measures. His infallibility bears upon the domain of thought, not directly of action . . .' (§ 10, p. 341). The domain of 'matters speculative', of 'thought', of 'religion'—in Newman's statement of the objection he was to answer—is the domain of doctrine. In this domain the pope teaches; in the other domain he requires things to be done, he commands. He can teach infallibly; he cannot command infallibly. No problem arises over Newman's assigning these two domains to the pope, with infallibility in one and authority in both: what the pope can do, and with what authority, has been ecclesiastically determined.

To conscience Newman assigns a single domain, that of our own conduct in the actual circumstances in which we find ourselves. Directing our conduct in these circumstances, all its deliverances on right and wrong are particular. It is their particularity that, in Newman's argument, insulates them against collision with infallibility. But how is this restriction on the scope of the deliverances of conscience justified? Newman is no more entitled merely to stipulate that 'conscience is not a judgment upon any speculative truth, any abstract doctrine, but bears immediately on conduct', on what is to be done or avoided here and now, than he is to stipulate that the pope is not infallible 'in his laws, nor in his commands'. We are about to take up the question of the justifiability of the restriction placed by Newman on the deliverances of conscience. But a problem which appears when the authority of conscience is brought into relation with the authority of the pope ought not to go unnoticed, though its discussion will have to wait.

The jurisdictional domain of the pope and the domain of conscience can intersect, and so there is the possibility of collision. The authority of the pope in his jurisdictional domain, though not infallible, is supreme, Newman has said. But he has also said that conscience has supreme authority over its domain. The problem will be discussed in the following chapter when what is to be *understood* by the ascription of authority to conscience is considered.

VI

We now look at Newman's argument which is to show that a collision between conscience and the infallibility of the Church—specifically that of the pope[26]—cannot take place. It occurs in the second of the numbered stages of his reply to the objection against the possibility of an independent Catholic conscience. The particularity of the deliverances of conscience is one of its premisses: conscience determines only what here and now, in these actual circumstances, is to be done as being right or to be avoided as wrong.[27] This premiss is not argued for but assumed. On what basis?

[26] No one would have insisted more strongly than Newman that there is only one infallibility, that of the Church, the pope under certain conditions being one channel of its exercise.

[27] That the deliverances of conscience are one and all particular was not rejected by implication when Newman called the moral law in the mind of each person 'conscience'. It was not implied that any of the deliverances of conscience have the generality of the contents of the moral law. Like his statement, at the same time, that the moral law is implanted by God in the intelligence of rational creatures (commented upon in § III of this chapter), this way of speaking is not to be pressed for its implications.

If (as was argued in the first chapter of this essay) any determination of right and wrong lies outside the conceptual boundaries of conscience; if, as regards doing and avoiding, its operation is only imperatival, coming into being when there is resistance within oneself or from others to the doing of something one takes to be right, or the avoiding of something taken to be wrong, the dictates of conscience will necessarily be particular, confined to the here and now. But as regards doing and avoiding, conscience for Newman is not confined to an imperatival particularity; to determine what ought to be done or avoided in particular cases comes within its domain. Why only in particular cases? Why does it not make general pronouncements on right and wrong? Newman perhaps inferred the particularity of all determination of right and wrong by conscience from what is a phenomenological fact, the invariable particularity of its imperatives. Another consideration might have been an inference from his perception that conscience is concerned 'with self alone and one's own action', which it would not be if it made general moral pronouncements. Inferences apart, he could not fail to be aware that it goes against the grain of the word to have conscience make such pronouncements.

Let it be allowed that the deliverances of conscience are always particular. How does Newman's argument then proceed to its conclusion? Judging only in fully particularized circumstances what is to be done as being good or avoided as evil, 'conscience cannot come into direct collision' with infallibility, for this is engaged on *general* propositions.[28]

---

[28] We can ignore the complication introduced by the engagment of infallibility also in the condemnation of errors (Letter, § 5, p. 256). In the condemnation of a proposition the Church's teaching is 'negatively' enunciated (see Letter to the Duke of Norfolk, § 9, pp. 332–4). In § 9 of the Letter a class of doctrines which are not 'general' is specified—those, like the doctrine of the Trinity, which 'relate to persons' (p. 334). (They, of course, equally with general moral propositions, come within the scope of an infallible pronouncement, and outside that of deliverances which bear 'immediately on conduct'.) With regard to the general doctrines an inference is drawn which has a very surprising initial appearance when thought of in relation to the moral teaching of the Church: in consequence of their being general, they 'admit of exceptions in their actual application'. One of the doctrines cited in illustration involves a moral proposition, the proposition implied in the condemnation of usury by an ecumenical council in the Middle Ages. Centuries later this condemnation might appear no longer to apply. Commenting on the change, Newman remarks that 'a double aspect seems to have been realized of the idea intended by the word *usury*'

It is not, however, a collision, simply, between conscience and infallibility that is thus inferred to be impossible: it is a 'direct' collision. What difference does Newman have in mind between a collision and a direct collision? Without an answer to that question, how he took the argument to work cannot be fully understood. Sharpening the question is the fact that, as though he had spoken of a collision simply, he immediately goes on to say 'Next, I observe that, conscience being a practical dictate, a collision is possible between it and the Pope's authority only when the Pope legislates, or gives particular orders, and the like', only in a domain, therefore, where there is no claim to infallibility. Supposing him, however, to have left open the possibility of an *indirect* collision between conscience and infallibility, what might he have had in mind?

Only one suggestion presents itself. Is the possibility of this indirect collision to be looked for in a procedure traditionally ascribed to conscience by Catholic moral theology, that of applying general moral propositions in particular circumstances? It is a promising suggestion in one way; in another it is not. Recommending it is its fitting in with Newman's remark quoted earlier, that the pope's infallibility 'bears upon the domain of thought, not directly of action'. A piece of moral teaching does not bear directly upon action: it has first to be applied in specific circumstances even if the application is obvious. But the suggestion does not look as though it would work. Conscience is to decide whether, say, a contemplated action is covered by the condemnation of all actions of such-and-such a kind as illicit. How could a decision of this nature collide in any way at all with the Church's teaching on the matter, a decision as to whether, under the circumstances, a certain action is of the kind specified by this teaching?

Exegetical defeat apart, it does not greatly matter in the end what Newman envisaged in his apparent contrast of a direct

(p. 337). These two aspects are, presumably, the usurious spirit and a practice embodying this spirit. And we can suppose Newman's thought in this example to have been that the transformation of the economic order since the Middle Ages required a largely different application of the pronouncement upon usury. In Newman's discussion of the three doctrines he cites to illustrate his statement that a general doctrine admits of exceptions in its application, the prominent point is the developed understanding of the doctrine which results from the drawing of distinctions.

with an indirect collision between conscience and infallibility, or whether he intended the contrast at all. Nothing that might bear on the contrast can abate the force of the collision that is possible, given a conception of conscience such as his, in which conscience determines the rightness or wrongness of what it commands or prohibits. It determines the rightness or wrongness only of actions in their concrete reality, and only of actions which will have oneself as their agent. Its determination of right and wrong is particular in every way. Notwithstanding this total particularity, its determination of right and wrong can come into head-on collision with some piece of the Church's teaching, and so with infallibility, notwithstanding the generality of this teaching.

Consider any piece of teaching condemning all actions of such-and-such a kind as wrong, and my rejecting the universality of this condemnation in the circumstances in which I am involved. It is not that I have decided that the condemnation does not apply to the action I am contemplating; I reject the condemnation in that instance. Remembering that conscience, as Newman depicts it, deals in opposites, in what must or must not be done—declaration that an action is morally permissible being absent from the picture—let us suppose that in the case we are considering the conviction reached is that the thing in question is right and so must be done. Now have it that it is conscience that pronounces the action to be right. Then the collision between this deliverance of my conscience and the teaching of the Church has the directness of a collision between a universal proposition and a contrary instance.

But with what justification is it held that conscience determines the rightness or wrongness of what it then commands or prohibits—conscience properly so called, conscience in the ordinary sense of the word? The conclusion to be drawn from the evidence we looked at is that no determination of right and wrong is undertaken by conscience, in the ordinary conception of it. It does not have, in this conception of it, the twofold operation, determinative as well as imperatival, it has in Newman's conception of it. Its dictates are purely imperatival, inward injunctions, tellings of oneself to do this, taken to be right or consciously judged to be so; not to do that, taken or judged to be wrong. If the dictates of conscience are purely imperatival, there is a conceptual parcelling out of activity as between one's conscience and oneself. A judgement of rightness or wrongness (capable of collision with what is laid down in moral teaching) is not made by my conscience, but by me; consequent upon this judgement, my conscience demands of me that the thing be done or avoided. The only participation of conscience in the making of the judgement, a participation which might be altogether implicit, is directed towards its being made with care and honesty—conscientiously.

Given that conscience, in the ordinary circumscribed conception of its activity, undertakes no determination of right and wrong, is the point of any significance, since a person, judging some piece of moral teaching to be mistaken, can in a perfectly intelligible, if extended use of the word, ascribe this judgement to his conscience? The point has all the significance we could want for our present concern, which is that there can be no collision between *conscience* and the Church's teaching. And for the time being that is sufficient.

But in Newman's conception of conscience the dictates of conscience are not purely imperatival. They incorporate a judgement made by conscience that a particular action is right or wrong. And so the possibility opens up of what appears to be a deadlocked encounter between conscience and infallibility.

VII

Is there perhaps more to Newman's conception of conscience than we have yet seen, which, when brought to light, would show that conscience and the Church's teaching are necessarily harmonious? There might seem to be a chance of our coming upon what would establish this harmony, in an account of Newman's view of the relation between conscience and the Church, given by John Coulson.

Our interpretation of the argument of the Letter to the Duke of Norfolk must rest upon a proper appreciation of the earlier argument

stated in the article 'On Consulting the Faithful in Matters of
Doctrine', and I refer in particular to Newman's distinction between
what he terms the phronesis and the phronema. Newman argues that
the power within us which is able to discern the difference between
right and wrong, which he terms the phronesis . . . is the counterpart
of 'that instinct, or phronema, deep in the bosom of the mystical
body of Christ'. . . [29]

Coulson is closer to the text of Newman's article, though still
reading beyond it, when he remarks (in the introduction to his
edition of the article) that this phronema in the Church, and
phronesis in the individual, are 'obviously' counterparts.[30] To
have seen them as counterparts results, in fact, from having
looked unifyingly into Newman's thought; for what Newman
says in the article with any obvious bearing on the matter is,
apart from a quoted reference to the 'conscience' of the
Church, as little as this:

I will set down the various ways in which theologians put before us
the bearing of the Consent of the faithful upon the manifestation of
the tradition of the Church. Its *consensus* is to be regarded: 1. as a
testimony to the fact of the apostolical dogma; 2. as a sort of instinct,
or φρόνημα, deep in the bosom of the mystical body of Christ
. . . 5. as a jealousy of error . . . (*On Consulting the Faithful*, p. 73)

Newman is defending his assertion that the laity are
'consulted' when the definition of a dogma is being prepared,
and so he is giving the opinions of theologians, not explicitly
his own opinion, in listing these points. In particular, the
word 'instinct', though his own word elsewhere and made his
own here, is borrowed. Included in the quotation amplifying
the second point, from Möhler (a theologian whose ideas on
the development of doctrine and Newman's were related), is
this set of expressions: '*un instinct* . . . qui . . . conduit à
toute vraie doctrine'; 'Ce sentiment commun, cette conscience
de l'Église'.[31]

---

[29] 'Conscience and Authority: Newman and the Two Vatican Councils', *Newman
Studien*, 9 (1974), 169.
[30] Newman, *On Consulting the Faithful in Matters of Doctrine*, ed. J. Coulson
(London, 1961), introd., 23.
[31] The conservative character of the 'consensus fidelium', in Newman's view of it,
is to be noticed. As giving testimony to what is traditional doctrine, it is necessarily
conservative, but as a doctrinal instinct it is conservative too; its 'jealousy of error' is
hardly an independent point on the list. In the article the laity are celebrated for

For material to fill out the claim that interpretation of the argument in the Letter to the Duke of Norfolk must rest upon what is to be found in this article, we turn to Coulson's book *Newman and the Common Tradition*. (After the passage quoted from 'Conscience and Authority' in which this interpretational dependency is stated, Coulson himself leaves the subject for matters more closely connected with his general theme.)

In *Newman and the Common Tradition*, as he had done earlier in his introduction to 'On Consulting the Faithful', Coulson associates with Newman's conception of conscience a principle uniquely important in his thought about the Church, a principle expressed in the words 'Securus judicat orbis terrarum.' In 1839, when the words were pointed out to him in St Augustine, they kept ringing in his ears as a judgement against the Church of England, no matter what the claims made for it, separated in actuality from the Catholic world;[32] and in 1870 they summarized for him the way in which doubts as to the validity of the Vatican Council would be settled. The principle they express is, of course, present in Newman's notion of the 'consensus fidelium'. This consensus, and a conscience whose deliverances were governed by the principle, would certainly be 'counterparts'.

Coulson contrasts Newman's view of conscience and of the Church with Lord Acton's (pp. 121–2). For Acton conscience was an 'individualizing faculty', and the Church, overwhelmingly, the scene of priestly action: conflict inevitable. To Newman a view of conscience such as Acton's 'allowed insufficiently for the limitations of the individual conscience which could claim infallibility only so far as it reflected the verdict of the whole world';[33] and to Newman, with his conception of the consensus fidelium, there was presented in the Church not an antagonist to conscience, but its counterpart.

keeping the faith during the rage of the Arian heresy when bishops and councils fell away. Quotations from Newman in Coulson's introduction to the article (pp. 46–7) strongly convey his sense that the danger to the Church of his times lay in an opposite direction from infidelity to doctrine, in the extent to which the spirit of another aberration of the past, the Novatianist schism, was gaining possession of it, a narrow sectarian spirit, 'trembling at freedom of thought', exalting its 'opinion into dogmas'.

[32] *Apologia*, ch. 3, p. 117.
[33] J. Coulson, *Newman and the Common Tradition* (Oxford, 1970), 121–2.

Newman saw 'the individual conscience (*phronesis*) as being fulfilled only in the *phronema*; or communal conscience of the whole Church: one was the mirror to the other, in which we could sometimes see ourselves more clearly, and by which our individual moral insights were fulfilled, completed, and sustained'. (*Newman and the Common Tradition*, p. 122).

We now appear to have before us everything of consequence that might be adduced to amplify the claim that interpretation of 'the argument' of the Letter to the Duke of Norfolk depends upon what is to be found in the article on consulting the faithful in doctrinal matters. The reference must be to the argument in the Letter bearing upon the relationship between conscience and the teaching of the Church; for the considerations to which our attention has been drawn, considerations involving individual and communal conscience, and the condition necessary for an infallible conscience (which Coulson apparently sees as an idea of Newman's) are not appropriate to the discussion in the Letter of conscience in relation to papal authority of a jurisdictional kind. What do these considerations suggest that would affect the interpretation of this argument? —*suggest*, for what Coulson takes their import to be in this precise connection is problematic. They suggest that, for Newman, a conscience in deadlocked collision with the teaching of the Church would have its title to the name withdrawn because subordination to the 'communal conscience' of the Church enters into the very notion of a believer's conscience; without this subordination to the mind of the Church or, at any rate, with this withheld, nothing in a believer, however much it might look like conscience, could be conscience.

Supposing that this did bring into view a latent element in Newman's conception of conscience, where would the interpretation of his argument be affected? The one possible place is where conscience 'truly so called' is distinguished from its counterfeit (Letter, § 5, pp. 250, 257–8). As Newman distinguishes them, the dictate of a conscience which is truly so called—of a conscience which is entitled to the name—presents itself to us as a demand on us from God; the counterfeit gives expression to a demand of self-will. Presupposed, then, by an authentic conscience are the right moral and religious dispositions (so far as self-scrutiny can tell). Included among these dispositions would be the disposition in a believer to conform to the mind of the Church. Required by the idea we are looking at is something different: actual conformity.

The idea is not Newman's. And, in themselves, the considerations that might suggest that it is are far more plausibly taken as intended to draw attention to a certain connaturality, in Newman's view, between conscience and the mind of the Church, and in doing this to show how strongly his conception of conscience is to be contrasted with one in which conscience is assuredly self-sufficient and naturally antagonistic to authority.[34] The difficulty, however, about taking them in an intrinsically plausible way is that, taken in this way, they leave the interpretation of the argument in the Letter to the Duke of Norfolk quite unaffected.

VIII

This argument was to establish the impossibility of collision between conscience and infallibility. The impossibility was to be established by showing their domains to be separate. Now that the possibility of their collision has opened up, the question arises whether, having said that there would be deadlock if it occurred, Newman can still maintain that conscience has supreme authority over our conduct?

The answer to a question which Newman had no occasion

---

[34] As pointing in the same direction, it might be added that Newman saw, for all its inwardness, a certain externality in conscience; the last thing its deliverances do, when he characterizes them, is present themselves as magnifying one's own point of view. The character of externality in the deliverances of conscience and a native orientation in it towards an authoritative teaching are brought together in one of Newman's sermons. In spite of all that the voice of conscience does for those who heed it, he says, 'it does not do enough'; but it 'inspires in them the idea of authoritative guidance'. Conscience 'by its very existence throws us out of ourselves, and beyond ourselves' (*Sermons on Various Occasions* (1857), No. 5, pp. 65–6). Newman did not, however, fail to see the contrary and more obvious tendency to which a preoccupation with conscience can give rise: 'Deference to the law of Conscience', he says in another sermon, 'is easily perverted into a kind of self-confidence, namely, a deference to our own judgment' (*University Sermons*, No. 9, p. 172).

to put to himself is that the deadlock can be broken in either of
two ways, each of them leaving the authority of conscience
unimpaired. In the situation produced by the collision the
infallibilist claims of the teacher are still acknowledged, while
at the same time something in the teaching is rejected as
mistaken. From this incoherence extrication is possible either
by a decision to accept the teaching or by a decision to reject
the teacher; neither will impugn the authority of conscience.

Consider what might go on in the mind of someone who
finds the judgement of his conscience, as he calls it,
inconsistent with the teaching of the Church. He might
remind himself of his belief in the Church's infallibility and
conclude as a matter of course, however painfully, that his
conscience had gone astray. Or, badly shaken, he might
review his grounds for this belief, perhaps reflecting at the
same time how easily conscience is 'obscured', how 'impressible' it is by current opinion, how 'unsteady in its course'; in
any case he ends up reaffirming his belief in the Church's
infallibility, and, as consistency requires, his conscience
comes round to the teaching it had rejected. If conscience is to
be credited with moral thinking at all, its first thoughts would
have no special title to being regarded as its privileged
declarations.[35] Is it objected that this concurrence in teaching
running counter to one's own thought would improperly be
described as an exercise of conscience? That is true, but not
for the reason implied in the objection, not because it is part of
the ordinary conception of conscience that conscience thinks
for itself; it is true because cogitation, ratiocination—like the
determination of right and wrong that would call for it—is not
engaged in by conscience at all. (Something will be said in the
following chapter relevant to the notion that a belief as to right
or wrong, of one's own, arrived at autonomously, carries an

[35] 'It is often said that second thoughts are best; so they are in matters of judgment,
but not in matters of conscience,' Newman writes at the end of a haunting sermon. 'In
matters of duty', he continues, 'first thoughts are commonly best—they have more in
them of the voice of God' (*Parochial and Plain Sermons*, iv, No. 2, p. 36). It would
be a misreading of Newman to see in these words an endorsement of the spontaneous
as opposed to the deliberative in moral thinking, as there could appear to be when
they are come upon in the absence of a context. The situation envisaged is this: you
were 'struck' at the time by something as coming from God; 'but somehow the more
you thought about it the less you liked or valued it'. The second thoughts Newman
speaks of are likely to be badly motivated.

imprimatur of conscience withheld from a belief made one's own by concurrence.)

It might happen, however, that the original judgement running contrary to the Church's teaching proves unalterable. And taking the judgement of his conscience to falsify the Church's claim to infallibility, a person might act accordingly and leave the Church. Instead, even though the teaching be such as to involve this claim paradigmatically, he might take it for one reason or another, or perhaps arbitrarily, to be something about which the Church could be mistaken, and remain an adherent; inconsistent in belief but in perfectly good conscience. Conscience does not have to be rational.

Conscience can have the final say over what one does, whatever one does. Go over the possibilities—all of them compatible with Newman's conception of conscience: conscience concurring, as a matter of course, or with an effort, in the Church's teaching; its withholding concurrence and there ensuing a rejection of the Church; its withholding concurrence and nothing ensuing. Conscience is not overriden, whichever takes place. And whichever takes place, the claim made by the Church is entirely unaffected.

5

ASCRIPTION OF AUTHORITY TO CONSCIENCE

THE authority of a conscience is not diminished for Newman by its being mistaken: not even by its being culpably mistaken, which it is when its error is due to some previous wilfulness or negligence on the part of the person whose conscience it is. For the conduct which has led him into error Newman of course sees him as responsible; 'but still he must act according to this error' while he takes it in 'full sincerity' to be truth.[1] The authority of conscience would not be diminished for Newman by a consensus of opinion against its judgement, no matter how general.[2] Involved in a clash even with the supreme authority of the pope, the authority of conscience is to prevail. There rests upon us in all circumstances 'the duty of obeying our conscience' (Letter, p. 250).

In corroboration of our being always bound to this obedience, Newman cites standard Catholic theological opinion. The language in the citations varies: conscience is ever 'to be obeyed'; there is 'sin' in disobedience to it; we are 'bound' to obey it; we have a 'duty' to obey it. This variation of language points to an opaqueness in the principle that is being expressed. The elucidation of the principle that conscience is always to be obeyed is a major concern of the present chapter. And it will be seen that this principle, though itself opaque, constitutes an important part of what is to be understood by Newman's ascription of authority to conscience.

---

[1] Letter to the Duke of Norfolk, § 5, p. 259.
[2] See Newman's letter to H. A. Woodgate, 23 Feb. 1872; *Letters and Diaries*, xxvi. 29. The letter contains important comment on the relation between individual judgement and general consent. It has a bearing on the matter of 'counterfeit intuitions' mentioned in ch. 3 n. 4 of this essay, and on the matter of conscience and the 'communal conscience' of the Church discussed in ch. 4, § VII.

That conscience has supreme authority over our conduct is obviously no idiosyncratic notion of Newman's in so far as the possession by conscience of this authority amounts to our having a never-failing duty to obey our conscience; for this principle carries great theological weight. It is not, however, only theologians and moralists who associate authority with conscience. The association sounds right to all of us—in spite of our being well acquainted with the failure to reach quite low standards of rationality that can lie behind the deliverances of conscience, and with the harm done by mistaken consciences. To these considerations, which make conscience as a bearer of authority something to be wondered at, should be added one more. Reaching no farther into the self than consciousness does (which is sometimes not as far as another's perception of us may reach), conscience can give no good guarantees against self-deception: behind its deliverances there may be adeptness in rationalization as well as defect in rationality. We shall remind ourselves of these considerations when we look at what makes appropriate the ascription of authority to conscience. It might very well turn out that what would be fatal to the possession by conscience of authority in any determination of right and wrong is irrelevant to its possession of imperatival authority.

We begin our enquiry into the ascription of authority to conscience with the variously expressed principle that conscience is always to be followed, that one has always a duty to obey one's conscience. There is a reason for spending time on the principle besides its importance for the subject of the present chapter. The question will come up in the next chapter whether Newman infers rights of conscience from the duty of following conscience. In that connection also, we shall want to know what is to be made of this 'duty'.

I

'Conscience is ever to be obeyed', 'Conscientia semper sequenda': one picks one's way through false appearances to an understanding of this principle. It looks at first sight as though its purpose might be to serve as a general reinforcement of the particular imperatives of conscience. Coming into being against resistance to the doing of what one takes to be right, this imperative can need all the strengthening it can get. 'Conscience must always be obeyed' might seem to be a strengthening injunction, addressed like the imperative of conscience itself, to the will. But if conscience is always to be obeyed, it is to be obeyed even when it is mistaken— 'Conscientia, etiam erronea, semper obligat.' Imagine, then, the words 'You must obey your conscience' addressed to someone being required by his conscience to do what the speaker regards as wrong. Urging someone to do something you yourself think wrong is a well-known kind of immoral behaviour, made worse by enlisting his conscience in the process. In this case, of course, you do not want the thing done, and you will have told the person you are now telling to obey his conscience that what he is contemplating is wrong. In effect you are telling him to do the thing you have told him not to do. Further, you certainly would not always, faced with any conceivable requirement of a conscience, urge on its possessor the need to obey his conscience; however indulgent you are to conscience, it would not be very long before you drew the line.

In its application to a mistaken conscience the principle that conscience is always to be followed can seem to generate a remarkable paradox. To have a mistaken conscience is to believe yourself required to do or refrain from something that is in reality morally indifferent, or to do something that is wrong, or not to do something that is right.[3] When the principle that conscience is always to be followed appears in the form that everyone is 'obliged' or has a 'duty' to obey his conscience even when it is mistaken, the paradox it can seem to generate becomes fully visible: that of being obliged or

---

[3] Mistakenly thinking that something wrong is not wrong, that it is permissible, would be a way of being mistaken in conscience, when the principle we want to understand is expanded so as to maintain that conscience must always be followed in what it requires, and may always be followed in what it allows. With this expansion of the principle we shall not concern ourselves. The discussion being entered upon now, and in the following chapter of the derivation of rights of conscience from the duty of obedience to conscience, will be unaffected. And in restricting ourselves to conscience as binding we shall be restricting ourselves to conscience as depicted by Newman.

having a duty to do a thing that is wrong, or not to do one that is right.

The familiar terms 'objective' and 'subjective' are put to an unfortunate use in a move that might be made, and perhaps quite often is made, to deal with the threat of this paradox. According to a familiar contrast, how things are objectively is how they are in fact, regardless of anyone's opinion; how they are subjectively is how they are in someone's belief about them. According to that contrast, one's having a 'subjective duty' to do or not to do whatever it is would be no more than one's believing oneself, truly or falsely, to have this duty. According to the distinction we are now considering, a 'subjective duty' is something altogether different. It is a *duty*—not a taking of oneself to have a duty. It is a duty brought into existence by this taking oneself to have the duty. And the suggestion seems to be that the paradox of a duty to do something wrong or not to do something right, which the principle that conscience is always to be followed can seem to generate, disappears with the realization that the duty and the rightness or wrongness are not on the same level; they are objective, the duty is subjective.

Obvious paradox is involved in this attempt to deal with a threatened paradox, in its crediting thought with the power to bring into existence as real a duty as an ordinary duty.

A note of hesitation, with regard to what we have been looking at, needs to be explained. The view that a mistaken conscience can create a duty which, for the agent, replaces the objective moral demands of his situation is one an exponent of the principle that conscience is always to be followed can quite strongly appear to hold when, dealing with its application to a mistaken conscience, he distinguishes between 'objective' and 'subjective' duty. But later on we shall come to an interpretation of the principle, threatening it with no paradoxical consequences, and this one would expect to be the implicit understanding of it even when things said in exposition of it suggest otherwise. So the view we looked at was not anybody's, but only a piece of conjecture. But there are actual, fully reflected upon assertions of the view that what the agent ought to do in any situation is what he thinks right, whether mistakenly or not. The particular interest of W. D. Ross's assertion of this view lies in an accompanying argument to show that it does not imply anything brought into existence by being thought to exist.

II

Ross distinguishes between an 'objective element' and a 'subjective element' in a situation in which it is necessary to act. The objective element 'consists of the facts about the various persons and things involved in the situation'—someone's state of need, for example—in virtue of which a certain act would be right; the subjective element consists of the agent's beliefs as to what these various matters of fact are.[4] This subjective element, it is to be noticed, does not correspond to anything in our discussion of a mistaken conscience in the previous section. In that discussion what could have been called the 'subjective element' was not any matter-of-fact belief of the agent, but his believing, given various matters of fact, that such-and-such an act was his duty. (Mistakes of quite different kinds—mistake as to some feature of the situation and mistake as to the moral demand of the situation—are covered by the indiscriminating notion of a mistaken conscience.)

Which of 'the two acts' is it that 'we ought to do', Ross asks, the act 'morally suitable' to the objective matter-of-fact features of the situation, or the act morally suitable to what these features are taken to be (p.147)? Setting out opposing considerations, he comes down in favour of the view that we ought to do the act suitable to what we take these features to be, the act suitable to 'the subjective facts of the situation'. But, as was pointed out in the discussion which Ross's ideas received, there is something wrong with the question. The agent could not ask himself, 'Which of these acts ought I to do?' because he is not able to step outside himself so as to be able to inspect the alternatives; necessarily, for him, the subjective facts of the situation coincide with the objective facts.

[4] W. D. Ross, *The Foundations of Ethics* (Oxford, 1939), 146.

The view recommending itself, at least at first sight, is that what we ought to do is made so by the objective facts of the situation. An objection to it put by Ross is its consequence that there could be things we ought to do without our knowing this; we might not know, for example, that our parents are in need and yet have a duty to help them. Why should that be an objection? A reason suggesting itself is the unfairness of having a duty when altogether ignorant of the circumstances giving rise to it. But this, or anything like it, would be a misconceived ground for the objection: no blame falls on a person for failing to meet an obligation in such a case, unless his ignorance is the result of negligence or worse.

So far the view put forward by Ross is that the act morally incumbent upon us is the act required by what we take to be the facts of our situation. His complete view is that what we are to do is what we take to be morally required by the circumstances, as we take them to be—'what the agent ought to do' in any situation is the act 'which he *thinks* to be morally most suitable in the circumstances' (p. 161), as these present themselves to him. The additional component of Ross's view corresponds to the proposition that we have a 'subjective' duty or obligation to act according to our conscience whether or not it is mistaken. Against this additional component of his view Ross brings the apparently fatal objection that it is 'clear on epistemological grounds that nothing can have a character simply by being thought to have it' (p. 162). The objection, he argues, is not in place. In none of three different kinds of rightness, of which the kind in question is the third, is anything made right, Ross contends, by being thought right:

In any particular situation in which a particular man is placed, there is one act which, if he had complete knowledge about the circumstances and a completely correct moral insight, he would see to be right in the first sense. There is no suspicion, even, of subjectivity in what is right in this sense. Secondly, suppose him to be mistaken about the circumstances; there is an act which is right in the second sense, in the sense of being appropriate to his opinion about the circumstances. That act is not made right in this second sense by being thought to be so; it bears the same sort of relation to the supposed situation as the first act does to the actual situation; the same kind of harmony exists in the one case as in the other;

the harmony is not created by being thought to exist, it exists independently of the agent's thought about it. Thirdly, the agent may be mistaken in his moral judgment of his duty in the supposed situation; but so long as he thinks as he does, the act in which he acts on his conviction has the same sort of harmony with his conviction as an act in which a man acts on a correct conviction has with that conviction, a harmony which is not created by his opinion but is there for all to apprehend. (pp. 164–5)

What *makes* the act right in the first of these cases? The facts as they objectively are. In the second? The facts as they are taken to be. And in the third case? There is nothing analogously right-making at all in the third case. The rightness here is of an altogether different kind from the other two. They attach to an act apart from its being done, as truth-telling, say, is right, whether or not people tell the truth. The rightness now in question is bound up with the act's being done, since it is a harmony between the agent's conviction as to what he should do and his actually doing it. Further demonstrating its anomalous character, this rightness obtains in the other two cases also—'the act in which he acts on his conviction has the same sort of harmony with his conviction as an act in which a man acts on a correct conviction has with that conviction'. It is certainly not a rightness brought into existence by being thought to exist. But while escaping the objection that there could be no such thing, it is unable to function in the way intended for it. Consider the question: 'Which act ought one to do, the objectively right act or this subjectively right act?' (We shall suppose, in order to make the point, the question not to be invalidated by a consideration similar to that invalidating the question reflected upon a moment ago, in which 'suitable to the objective circumstances', 'suitable to the subjective circumstances', are the alternatives.) Since the rightness we are looking at is a harmony between a belief and the act *done* in accordance with the belief, it is not a kind which could attach to an action *to be done*. Reference to it is therefore out of place in a question asking which act ought one to do. It is a kind of rightness altogether different from the rightness being defended against the objection that nothing exists in virtue of being thought to exist.

III

We return to the principle that conscience is always to be followed, and resume the matter of its interpretation. Construe the principle in its reference to a mistaken conscience as pronouncing upon the rectitude of the agent, and not at all upon some rightness attaching to an act, and no paradox is generated. It is possible to act with the right disposition, whether or not the act itself is right, so long as it is thought right. There is no need for more than this thinking; absolutely no need for it to bring into existence a species of rightness—'subjective rightness', or a species of duty—'subjective duty'. And it is likely that this is how, as a rule, the principle is construed (with varying degrees of clarity) even when such terms make an entry into its exposition or into some application of it, and suggest otherwise. Thus construed, it would authorize an exculpatory judgement on a person for his action, like that made by Newman explaining something he had said about obedience to a culpably mistaken conscience: a person, he says in the course of this explanation, incurs no guilt for acting according to such a conscience. ('He is guilty not for his act, but for his state of mind.')[5] The principle will also authorize a condemnatory judgement. To disobey conscience is to sin, Aquinas maintains. And asking in the *De Veritate* whether a mistaken conscience 'binds', and answering that it does, he explains what is meant by conscience 'binding'. It is that by disobeying his conscience a person sins.[6]

We are now in a position to see what the principle that conscience is always to be followed amounts to. It amounts to the two propositions: that guilt is never incurred by a person acting as he thinks right, and that guilt is always incurred by a person failing to act as he thinks right, or acting in a way he thinks wrong.

From the second of these propositions the principle would derive its imperatival force in application to a conscience assumed *not* to be mistaken. To bring out again how

---

[5] Newman to Bishop Moriarty, 6 Mar. 1875; *Letters and Diaries*, xxvii. 241.

[6] *De Veritate*, Q. 17, A. 4; cf. *Summa Theologica*, 1a2ae, Q. 19, A. 5, where it is implied that for a mistaken conscience to bind is for there to be 'badness of the will' in transgression against it.

inappropriately it would be applied with imperatival force to situations in which a person is regarded as mistaken in conscience, let us vary a point made earlier. You have, suppose, told someone that his conscience is mistaken (it will not have been a bare telling, you will have reasoned with him), and then perhaps you say to him that he must obey his conscience. One thing you might be doing with these words is giving him up, abandoning him to his conscience. Only in exceptional circumstances (worried, it might be, by the guilt he would feel if he went against his conscience), and not thinking the thing contemplated very bad, would you have any intention of getting him to obey his conscience. Obviously, he could not himself say that he must obey his conscience though it was mistaken. He could say that he must obey it though it might be mistaken. He would not be reinforcing its imperative. The import of his words would seem to be, self-reassuringly, that faced with a requirement of his conscience, he was left with no choice and would deserve no blame, if what he was going to do turned out to have been wrong.

IV

The traditional theological setting of the principle that conscience must always be obeyed—one's accountability before God—invites its being seen as a general authorization of particular judgements, exculpatory and condemnatory, which foreshadow the Last Judgement. That Judgement is of course wholly retrospective, on persons, for what they have done or left undone. 'Conscience must always be obeyed' has a strong prospective appearance, appears to dictate that the action thought right be done. This appearance is illusory, we argued, when the principle is considered in reference to a mistaken conscience. It helps to explain, however, what in itself is so surprisingly said, that there is an 'obligation' or a 'duty' to obey a *mistaken* conscience.

In everyday life we are pulled in opposite directions in passing judgement on those who, obeying a conscience we think mistaken, have done harm. Equity seems to require that nobody be condemned for acting according to what light he has. Utilitarian considerations support and counteract this consideration. We have a good reason for endorsing the general rule that conscience is to be obeyed. To get people to do what they would admit they ought to—that is the usual need; conscience is dangerous only once in a while, though when it is we are apt to think it is something we would be better off with less of. Our policy is to foster obedience to conscience, but we want people to learn to be careful about what their conscience requires of them when others are going to be affected. The result of these considerations seems to be a disposition to have a mistaken conscience exculpate—always, of course, within limits. If we condemn someone who has not followed a conscience we regard as mistaken, we would condemn him, wouldn't we?, not precisely for that, but for pusillanimity or something of the sort.

Utilitarian considerations drop away when grounds are sought for the principle that conscience must always be obeyed, viewed in its theological setting. Underlying the principle is what presents itself as the most fundamental of moral requirements, namely that the will be conformed to what is perceived as right. The additional, distinctively theological, grounding of the principle is direct and oblique. Direct, with Aquinas; oblique, with Newman.

In the view which Aquinas could take for granted the imperative of conscience comes as communicating the command or prohibition of God, so that disobedience to conscience has forthwith the character of disobedience to God. Blocked from being able to disobey God by the circumstance that his conscience is mistaken and so misrepresents this command or prohibition, a person disobeying his conscience disobeys God 'as far as he is able to'.[7] The background to this view is an age in which God commanding what is right and prohibiting what is wrong is as much a fact to its consciousness as right and wrong themselves are. Newman's oblique theological grounding of the authority of conscience belongs to a different age, when the thought of God is absent or dim. So a beginning is made with the phenomena of

---

[7] *De Veritate*, Q . 17, A. 4.

conscience. And their 'testimony' is evoked: to God 'as a reality'; to God as ruler and as one's judge.

Though the age of Aquinas has passed away with its taken-for-grantedness that there is a God, and that what is right is commanded by God and what is wrong forbidden, it has in this respect a reproduction in every individual believing in God as a reality. Such a believer sees the demand of his conscience that he do or avoid the thing taken to be right or wrong as directly invested with authority from God. And Newman, of course, would see it thus. He gives the authority of conscience an oblique theological grounding when he is showing how one becomes such a believer.

The long-enduring theological aura of conscience will have contributed by various channels of influence to a sense, even in secularized minds, that it has an authority which nothing can impugn. Even as a mere linguistic relic, the metaphor in which conscience is the voice of God will contribute to this effect.

V

It is the imperatival authority of conscience that has been under consideration, the authority of conscience as commanding and prohibiting, not any authority it might have in determining what to command and prohibit, supposing this to be something it does. And a point come upon in the course of the discussion suggests a reason, additional to our experience of the magisterial character of the dictate of conscience, why nothing seems able to diminish this authority, though conscience can give no good guarantee against self-deception, though behind its imperative there may be irrationality and culpable mistake. The imperative of conscience is experienced when there is resistance to the doing of what is perceived as right. The imperative of conscience is directed towards bringing the will into conformity with this perception when it does not spontaneously conform to it. That there be this conformity seems simply obvious if morality is to exist at all; and the sense of its necessity would contribute to an explanation as to how it is that conscience has come to be credited with having a unique authority. None of the disqualifications which present themselves to the idea of conscience as a bearer of authority touch an authority derived from the need for the will to be conformed to what is seen as right.

Altogether independent of how what is taken to be right or wrong is arrived at, the imperatival authority of conscience does not destow any cachet on one's having judged for oneself instead of having deferred to someone else's judgement, or to the authority of some institution. An obvious point, but there is a reason why it should be mentioned. Individuality is deeply involved in the notion of conscience. No one's conscience pronounces upon or for others. Conscience does not have the impersonality of one's reason. And so it might be imagined that conscience irradiates with itself what is personal in thinking about right and wrong, in some way conferring its own prerogatives on moral thinking that is autonomous. It would dispel the imagination to ask what these conferred prerogatives might be: some special deference due to one's own moral opinion because it is one's own, not adopted from someone else thought to be a better judge? an inviolability, even, attaching to it because it is one's own? Certainly, there is a common enough use of the word 'conscience' in which going by one's own conscience is contrasted with adopting someone else's opinion. An example is Newman's saying (in connection with a hypothetical case involving his duty as a citizen and his duty to the pope): 'I should look to see what theologians could do for me . . . what friends . . . and if, after all, I could not take their view of the matter, then I must rule myself by my own judgment and my own conscience.' There is, of course, no conceptual oddity, nor any indication of moral weakness, in Newman's speaking of being driven back on his own conscience as a last resort.

VI

We now consider the ascription of authority to conscience thought of as determining right and wrong; first the view to be found in Newman; in the next section, the idea itself.

Only in one place in the account Newman gives of conscience based on its phenomena is there anything that might suggest he saw it as having authority in the determination of right and wrong he assigned to it. Conscience

vaguely reaches forward to something beyond self, and dimly discerns a sanction higher than self for its decisions, as is evidenced in that keen sense of obligation and responsibility which informs them. And hence it is that we are accustomed to speak of conscience as a voice . . . and moreover a voice, or the echo of a voice, imperative and constraining, like no other dictate in the whole of our experience.[8]

In this passage it is said that one's conscience discerns a 'sanction' higher than oneself for its *decisions*, and this might suggest that it is being represented as feeling some divine authorization for its judging this to be right, that to be wrong. There is nothing in Newman's phenomenology of conscience that would correspond to this suggestion. Its subject is an ordinary conscience, and any such feeling, even if not intense, would be rare;[9] unless you were an unusual sort of person, you would not often feel, however religious you might be, that your settling on something or other as the right thing to do was God-directed. Evidencing the sanction attached to 'decisions' of conscience is said to be the sense of obligation and responsibility with which they are informed. By the end of the passage, however, it has become clear—as it is elsewhere in the account of conscience based by Newman on its characteristic feelings and states of mind—that the sense of obligation with its transcendent warrant is related, not to any deciding upon something as right, but to the doing of what has been decided upon as right. At the beginning of the passage the two aspects, decisional and imperatival, of the 'indivisible' act of conscience are not kept distinct; and the decisional aspect appropriates what belongs to conscience in its 'primary and most authoritative aspect'.

If, then, the sanction higher than oneself for the dictates of

---

[8] *Grammar of Assent*, ch. 5, § 1, p. 107.

[9] The experience described in one of the *University Sermons* is surely of no ordinary occurrence: a conscience which has been trifled with becomes 'irregular' in moral judgement; whereas in someone who is always sensitive to his conscience, 'what was as uncertain as mere feeling, and could not be distinguished from a fancy except by the commanding urgency of its voice, becomes fixed and definite' (*University Sermons*, 3rd edn., No. 5, p. 81).

conscience, as evidenced by the sense of obligation which informs them, attaches to them as imperatival, what for Newman invests conscience with authority in its decisional aspect? Realization that it might be hard to find an answer is brought on when, in the words just now quoted, Newman calls one aspect more authoritative than the other. The attempt to think out the notion of degrees of authority here leads quickly to questioning the appropriateness of any ascription of authority to conscience in the determination of right and wrong. Let us, however, look at what Newman has to say in the Letter to the Duke of Norfolk about the foundation of 'the supreme authority of conscience'. Conscience is an implantation in us of the Divine Law. The Divine Law is

the rule of ethical truth, the standard of right and wrong, a sovereign, irreversible, absolute authority . . . 'The eternal law,' says St. Augustine, 'is the Divine Reason or Will of God, commanding the observance, forbidding the disturbance, of the natural order of things.' 'The natural law,' says St. Thomas, 'is an impression of the Divine Light in us, a participation of the eternal law in the rational creature.' . . .This law as apprehended in the minds of individual men, is called 'conscience;' and though it may suffer refraction in passing into the intellectual medium of each, it is not therefore so affected as to lose its character of being the Divine Law, but still has, as such, the prerogative of commanding obedience. (§ 5, pp. 246–7)

It might seem from the end of the passage that authority is being ascribed to conscience as an implantation of the Divine Law, altogether in virtue of its imperatival character, but complete symmetry is probably intended: the pronouncements that this is right, that wrong, made by conscience, though possibly erroneous, correspond to the content of the Divine Law; the imperative of conscience corresponds to the imposition of this upon us as *law*. But it is hardly to be supposed that Newman thought that anything in this correspondence conferred authority on the intellectual medium by which the Divine Law is apprehended, on the process from which the pronouncements emerge. So we are no further towards understanding why he ascribed authority to conscience in the determination of right and wrong.

We shall not be brought any closer to an understanding by considering Newman's juxtaposition of the authority of conscience with an authority whose rationale he could perfectly explain, papal authority. In a conflict between conscience and 'the supreme, though not infallible Authority of the Pope', the dictate of conscience prevails (Letter, § 5, pp. 257–8). The command of conscience prevails against a papal injunction; one acts according to one's conscience and not as the pope directs, obeys one's conscience and not the pope. As the language indicates, the authority that is pitted against the authority of the pope is the imperatival authority of conscience.[10] The imperatival authority of conscience, however, is not our concern now; our interest is in an authority possessed by conscience determining what to command and prohibit. There are grounds for the dictate of a person's conscience that he must not do as the pope requires. Is it to be supposed that in some way authority attaches to the marshalling of these grounds by conscience? We shall consider the question in relation to one of the examples of a possible collision between conscience and the pope, mentioned but not developed by Newman. In this example the pope calls on Catholics to refuse to serve in their country's armed forces in a war which he has condemned as unjust, is disagreed with over the justice of the war, and disobeyed.

When the legitimacy of disobedience to a papal command is at issue, it must be remembered, Newman remarks, that obedience to the pope is the rule and that, consequently, 'the *onus probandi* of establishing a case against him lies, as in all cases of exception, on the side of conscience' (Letter, p. 258). Newman does not say that conscience makes out the case against the pope. Could he have been expected to? Why not, since he maintains that implicit reasoning is an activity of conscience, and that it is for one's conscience to judge the

---

[10] In his juxtaposition of the authority of conscience with that of the pope the path-finding ability of conscience is not an issue raised by Newman. Consequently, a very misleading impression as to what Newman was claiming here for conscience is produced when, in a summary of his position, he is represented as maintaining that we are to be *guided* by conscience: 'The general lines . . . are well known . . . Conscience is the supreme guide to action' (David Nicholls, 'Gladstone, Newman and Pluralism', in *Newman and Gladstone: Centennial Essays*, ed. James Bastable (Dublin, 1978), 32–3).

morally right thing to do in a situation where one has to do something? But inhibiting his saying that conscience makes out the case against the pope is the unnaturalness of saying it. A conscience adducing considerations and reaching a conclusion on the basis of their combined significance, however implicit its reasoning, would be a conscience intolerably personified. Newman gave no examples of the engagement of conscience in implicit reasoning. The fact is that an attempt to produce an example brings out the resistance latent in the ordinary conception of conscience to having conscience engage in any ratiocinative operation.

But let conscience reason. Its reasoning in the matter supposed would traverse two areas, one related to the justice of the war (how the war came about would be an issue), the other to the range and gradations of papal authority. What could be meant by any suggestion that authority attaches to its deliberations in these areas?

From a practical perspective it is a good thing that conscience is thought able to reason if it is thought able to determine right and wrong. For, familiar with the way in which conscience works, those who think of their moral decisions as made by their conscience are exposed to some risk of basing these decisions on mere feeling. A further point of practical significance to be noticed is that the ascribing of authority to conscience in the determination of right and wrong weakens the protection derived from its being thought able to reason. For we do not associate the notion of authority with reasoning. The appropriate deliverances for a conscience viewed as having authority in the determination of right and wrong would be oracular.

Looked at together, two things said by Newman in connection with a collision between conscience and the pope, while they have no tendency to render questionable the ascription of imperatival authority to conscience, strongly point to the need for elucidation. They come one after the other, though there is a variation in context. Concluding his argument to show that the dictate of conscience can override a papal injunction, Newman says, 'the Pope is not infallible in that subject-matter in which conscience is of supreme authority' (Letter, § 5, p. 257). The subject-matter in which conscience has supreme authority is one's own conduct in actual situations. Newman goes on to specify the conditions (bearing on the integrity of conscience) that must obtain when conscience has 'the right of opposing the supreme, though not infallible Authority of the Pope' (p. 257). The subject-matter of this authority is an ecclesiastically determined part of the conduct of those, among them oneself, under the pope's rule. It includes part of the conduct over which one's conscience was said to have supreme authority.

There is no inconsistency in Newman here. There would be if the same thing had been meant when supreme authority in a collision was ascribed to both conscience and the pope; and, of course, it was not. The pope has authority in a wholly non-figurative sense. Figurative language starts up almost as soon as conscience is spoken of: personifying figure, reifying figure, a panoply of legal metaphor; and the ascription of authority to conscience is of a piece with this. A meaning does not have to be looked for when authority is ascribed to the pope; it has to be looked for when authority is ascribed to conscience. Newman does not announce any elucidation, but he provides one when, looking back on the outcome of his discussion of conflict between conscience and the pope, he speaks of 'the duty of obeying our conscience at all hazards' (p. 259). These words would give a natural meaning to his asserting that conscience has supreme authority over what each of us does in a context in which, over part of our conduct, the supreme authority of the pope is also asserted. The meaning would be that we have always an overriding duty to obey our conscience.

The principle which Newman's words express, however, itself needs elucidation. And the 'duty to obey' undergoes a great transmutation of meaning when this principle is construed not as pronouncing upon what is to be done, but upon how we are to be judged when we act in accordance with or contrary to our conscience. Interpreted in this way, the principle provides a much less obvious basis for an ascription of authority to conscience than in its uninterpreted formulation. The loss is not very significant, however, for Newman can be seen to base the ascription of authority to conscience primarily on the magisterial character of its commands and prohibitions.

We have come upon nothing to make understandable the

notion of an authority possessed by conscience in the determination of right and wrong. And on reflection it can seem to be a notion which one has read into Newman. The clearest indication that he entertained it is a remark which indicates how little it was thought through: the remark in which the determinative aspect of conscience appears as less 'authoritative' than its magisterial aspect.

VII

Independently of anything that might be found in Newman, let us look further at the notion of conscience as having authority in the determination of right and wrong. And in order to see more clearly, let us break off talk of conscience as engaging in this enterprise and think instead of oneself as doing so. Where does any notion of authority come into view? Where is there any of the subordination involved in that notion? How different the situation is from any in which it would be appropriate to speak of self-command, say, or of bringing oneself to do something, which are analogous to, or coincident with, features of being governed by conscience. Revert to speaking of conscience as determining right and wrong. The name comes with its magisterial sound but is given an empty application; except in so far as it would imply that the operation is being conducted conscientiously, that is with due care. More seems to be indicated than the ground-lessness of the ascription of authority to conscience in any determination of right and wrong. The ascription of authority to conscience in this connection looks to be without meaning.

Might not conscience, though, have an authority here which is not structured like its authority of command and prohibition, but which can as little be gainsaid? Let us see if we can find what we are looking for among the considerations brought by Bernard Mayo (one of the few comparatively recent British philosophers to have given the notion of conscience any prominence) to show that 'the authority of conscience is ultimate and unchallengeable'.

Dismissing the idea that the word 'conscience' names a

faculty or some 'psychical component' of our nature, Mayo
describes its function as being 'to figure in expressions which
refer to the issuing of self-directed commands in accordance
with moral rules which we adopt as authoritative'.[11] The
briefly stated grounds on which he goes on to ascribe ultimate
authority to conscience are these: 'one can challenge an
authority only by appeal to some other authority, so that one
must rest somewhere with a decision to accept some ruling as
final; and this decision will be a moral decision and conscience
the final and ultimate authority.' (p. 171)

The first thing to be noticed is that it is not true that an
authority can be challenged only by appeal to another
authority. Sometimes an appeal is made from one authority to
another; in an example of Mayo's, from the authority to one's
school teacher forbidding make-up to the authority of one's
parents who allow it. Notably, however, one may reject an
authority, not by invoking against it another authority, but by
rejecting its credentials. Thus, someone might come to reject
the claims of his Church and therefore its authority, on the
ground that it no longer behaved as if it believed its own
claims. If we think that an authority can be challenged only by
appeal to another authority, then looking round for an
authority where none exists, we are likely to make false
investitures of authority.

At the beginning of Mayo's argument conscience is assigned
a function which is genuinely authoritative in character, that
of issuing commands in accordance with moral rules which we
adopt. *We* adopt the rules; conscience does not have a hand in
this matter, according to what is stated at the beginning of the
argument. The rules we adopt are quite naturally said to be
'authoritative', since they have a governing role in relation to
our behaviour. ('The authority of a moral rule appears in the
agent's readiness to obey a command, derived from the rule,
and issued by himself to himself' (p. 168). It is difficult to
work out how the argument goes after conscience is assigned
its imperatival function. The authority challengeable only by
appeal to 'some other authority' seems to be that of the moral
rule or principle. What is the other authority here? It might
seem to be the moral principle in competition with the one

[11] Bernard Mayo, *Ethics and the Moral Life* (London, 1958), 171.

being called into question. But a 'ruling' is spoken of, and a principle is not competent to give that. There is nothing in the picture, except conscience, which looks as though it might be able to give a ruling; we ourselves, not possessing any sort of authority, can only decide between the competing principles. But if conscience gives a ruling, the expectation is that it would impose this on us, as befits an exercise of authority. In Mayo's text, however, we decide to accept the ruling as final. And to have conscience give a ruling, is to have it take on a function beyond that originally assigned to it, which was to command and prohibit in accordance with our moral rules.

There is some further material which needs to be taken into account before a summarizing interpretation of the argument is attempted. It can be remarked at this point, though, that a switch from speaking of our adopting a principle to speaking of our conscience as ruling in its favour would bring with it no accession of meaning. Contrast this empty change to a way of speaking in which 'conscience' is used with nothing of its distinctive meaning with an example of the substantial loss of meaning in a paraphrase: contrast the substitution of 'self-directed commands and prohibitions' for 'commands and prohibitions of conscience'. Self-directed imperatives are not peculiar to conscience; they are delivered by the Himalayan climber, for instance, urging himself on. (The 'internalizing' of any rule can occasion them, Mayo points out.) Nor would 'self-directed imperatives' be adequately specified as imperatives of conscience by the addition of some such phrase as 'in accordance with moral rules', for the imperatives of conscience bear on religious duty and transgression as well as moral. It might even turn out that there is no specification of 'self-directed imperatives' which would make them quite coincident with the imperatives of conscience. (This is to be expected if Newman is right in saying that the dictate of conscience is 'like no other dictate in the whole of our experience'.)

To return to the interpretation of Mayo's argument. It would take a reader totally by surprise if he had to understand the implication of 'one must rest somewhere with a decision to accept some ruling as final' to be that conscience gave rulings between competing moral principles. Consistently, in what has gone before, *we* adopt or make up our minds about moral principles, simply; there is no place for any sort of intervention by conscience in the process, all it does is to command or prohibit in accordance with a principle once this is adopted. A later passage, making it as plain as can be that conscience is not thought of as having any role in the adopting of moral principles, has it, however, give them subsequent authority. Conscience 'gives authority to whatever set of rules one does in fact adopt; and if one chooses to adopt a different set of rules . . . one does not reject conscience, but only certain rules' (p. 175). It is, presumably, by commanding and prohibiting in accordance with the rules that conscience gives them authority.

An interpretation of the argument to show that conscience has 'ultimate and unchallengeable authority' can now be proposed which meets all the demands of the text, except the mention of a ruling. It would run as follows: Conscience, as holding us in our behaviour to conformity with moral principle (regardless of what we might like to do on any occasion), has authority over our behaviour. And its authority is ultimate and unchallengeable because no matter what moral principles we adopt, conscience will issue commands and prohibitions to us accordingly. Recommending this interpretation is its giving real content to the notion of conscience as having authority—the content we have become familiar with, however—which is not now our interest.

We were looking for some justification for attaching the notion of authority to conscience assigned a decision-reaching or determinative role in matters of right and wrong. A different kind of authority from its imperatival authority would be involved; not that of someone *in* authority, that of someone who *is* an authority. And in matters of right and wrong no ordinary person is that. Aristotle's man of practical wisdom might be said to be such, but there is no pointer here to any justification for ascribing authority of the kind being considered to routine consciences, which is what is needed.

Does the objection, put on behalf of a determinedly reifying conception of conscience, have to be met, that in some way a conscience might have this authority, though its possessor does not? It could be left to the objector to produce some ground for the distinction between himself and his conscience in this connection, to show that he is not simply choosing to say that his conscience decides upon or determines right and wrong instead of that he does. But a reason might as well be given for denying any reality to the distinction. Sometimes the conclusion is reached that a thing is right or wrong, sometimes its being one or the other strikes us as obvious: an instrumentality correspondingly diverse in its operations would be a fairly patent fiction.

We might just glance at the notion that everyone's conscience has authority in decisions on right and wrong quite simply in virtue of its having the last word. To get the notion going at all there is needed the habit of thinking of these decisions as made by one's conscience. Then an ambiguity in 'the last word' might make it seem plausible. When a person makes a judgement on right and wrong which involves his accepting or rejecting what someone else, or an institution, has to say, he has the last word, the final say. But while it certainly belongs to the notion of an ultimate authority to have the last word on matters falling within its domain, there is nothing authoritative about the last word on matters of right and wrong we all have—which our conscience has, if that is how we are going to talk—any more than there is about the last word which someone gives himself when he breaks off a discussion. In one kind of situation, having to decide, we might decide to accept some piece of teaching though it runs counter to what we would have thought ourselves, because it is imposed by an authority whose claims we accept. This submission is not the act of an authority which is somehow higher than the external authority. Nor would rejection of the teaching have been that.

VIII

No justification for attaching any notion of authority to conscience thought of as determining right and wrong has appeared. And only if conscience had this determinative role would it have, and then only in that role, the disqualifications as a bearer of authority we were to keep in mind—vulnerability to self-deception, and the fact that behind what would be its deliverances there may lie culpable mistake and any degree of irrationality—disqualifications which, since they are related to the ascertaining of truth, are irrelevant to conscience in its imperatival role.

The ordinary conception of conscience provides a basis for the ascription of authority to conscience, but not in the determination of right and wrong. It provides this in its representations of conscience as commanding that what is taken to be right be done and what is taken to be wrong avoided, and of conscience as passing judgement on a person for his actions. Once the notion of authority is attached to conscience, however, there is an obvious explanation, as distinct from a justification, for its being readily supposed that conscience has authority in the determination of right and wrong. 'Conscience' is widely used to designate the source of convictions on right and wrong. How likely that so powerful a word would carry its magisterial aura with it when it is used in this way, and that when conscience is taken to be the source of these convictions, it will unreflectingly be felt to be their authoritative source.

We can now take up a postponed question. If conscience, in the ordinary conception of it, engages in no determination of right and wrong, if its dictates are purely imperatival, its collision with anything in the Church's teaching is impossible. The question we were to take up is whether there is any significance in this impossibility, since one can certainly do oneself what conscience would be conceptually barred from doing, and the doing of it can be ascribed in a perfectly intelligible, if extended, use of the word, to one's conscience. Its significance is that if conscience is seen as a party to the confrontation, the picture is easily formed of authority confronting authority. The reality misrepresented by this picture is authority on one side and, on the other, merely one's dissenting self, with an opinion no weightier than the reasons one might have for it.

IX

The notion of conscience as having authority, however much it answers to our feelings about conscience, belongs in the first instance to the discourse of theologians and moralists, not to our everyday untheoretical talk about conscience. Accordingly, we have to be told or find out what we are to understand by the notion. And this may vary widely from one writer to another.[12] The question as to what Newman meant by the authority of conscience arises sharply, as we have seen, from the circumstance that when two things said by him are brought together, both conscience and the pope have 'supreme authority' in a domain where collision between them is possible.

What is to be understood by the authority of conscience in its juxtaposition with that of the pope is suggested when Newman goes on to assert 'the duty of obeying our conscience at all hazards': the authority of conscience and this duty amount to the same thing. Prior to this duty, however, is something Newman sees as foundational to it, though again the connection is suggested rather than stated. Foundational to the duty of obedience to conscience is the magisterial character of the dictate of conscience. And perhaps nothing else ever written does so much to explain how it comes about that the notion of authority clings to the idea of conscience, as is done by the phenomenological account of conscience, centring on this dictate, which is given in the *Grammar of Assent*; though to explain why authority is associated with the idea of conscience was not Newman's purpose, though the only mention of authority occurs in the remark that the aspect of conscience being described is its 'primary and most authoritative aspect'. Described for our recognition as what we find within ourselves are phenomena which make it appropriate to speak of conscience as commanding and prohibiting actions, as attaching sanctions to its commands and prohibitions, and as passing judgement upon us for our actions— representations of conscience to which the notion of authority inevitably unites itself. To the extent that Newman's description

---

[12] Any feeling that there must be a standard account of the authority of conscience ought to be dissipated by so striking a divergence of view as the following: we 'credit conscience with *authority*' because 'its exercise is behaving or trying to behave' in accordance with moral convictions, Ryle says (*Collected Papers*, ii. 188), bringing the authority of conscience into alignment with its *power*, which Butler (*Sermons*, No. 2, p. 64) contrasts with its authority—'had it power, as it has manifest authority; it would absolutely govern the world.' For Butler the authority of conscience is its entitlement, derived from the constitution of our nature, to govern our conduct.

of these phenomena meets with our further recognition, they convey to us a sense, however inarticulate, of the correspondence of conscience, in its commanding and prohibiting of actions and in its judgements upon us, with God as ruler and judge, a sense therefore of the correspondence of its authority with ultimate authority.

We found nothing that looked like rendering appropriate the ascription of authority to conscience in any determination of right and wrong it might be supposed to undertake. We were, in fact, unable to make sense of the notion. Much of our attention in this chapter was concentrated on the principle that conscience is always to be followed, on an attempt to reach an understanding of it rather than on the matter of its justification. Applied in the case of a 'mistaken conscience', as it is called, the principle can seem to generate the paradox that a duty exists to do something wrong, or not to do something that is right. Reasons were given against attempting to dispose of the paradox by means of a distinction between 'objective' and 'subjective' duty or obligation. The paradox arises because the principle that conscience is always to be followed has the illusory appearance of dictating the *action* to be done. The line of interpretation we adopted was to take it to have, at least as its main concern, the judgement to be passed on a *person* acting, or failing to act, as his conscience requires. So understood the principle has in part an exculpatory import: it maintains that no guilt is incurred for an action done in accordance with a mistaken conscience. It also maintains that guilt is incurred for all action or inaction at variance with one's conscience, mistaken or not. Only in its exculpatory import, grounds were seen for thinking, does this principle of moral theology express our everyday attitude towards actions proceeding from a conscience we regard as mistaken.

6

'RIGHTS' OF CONSCIENCE

THE impression exists that Newman's teaching on conscience requires that great latitude be extended to conscience when it runs up against authority, civil or religious. In some of the talk about conscience, especially when either of two very solemn locutions enters into it, 'the inviolability of conscience', 'the sacrosanctity of conscience' (neither of them to be found in Newman, so far as one has noticed), the rights of conscience are pitched very high. In a paper presented to a recent Newman conference Newman is made to sponsor as extreme a claim for the rights of conscience as any that could be made. Newman's attention was 'focused on the question of supremacy or primacy of conscience', the writer remarks, 'rather than on freedom of conscience'; but conscience was 'inviolable' to him. And if

his personal experiences of the obligation of the supremacy of his conscience are considered, it can be seen that he took for granted the fact that, because he was absolutely bound by a judgment of his conscience, and had the duty to put it into effect, other people or authorities did not have the right to impede him or force him in any way. This freedom is such that he could not be forced to act against his conscientious judgment or be restrained from acting in accordance with it.[1]

Of course Newman did not take such a notion for granted; of course he would have thought us entitled to protect ourselves against a conscience on the rampage. But of course it does not follow from the fact that Newman would have repudiated this notion of a limitless freedom for conscience, that it is without foundation somewhere in his teaching about conscience. Its

---

[1] John Jago, 'J. H. Newman and Freedom of Conscience', in *Shadows and Images*, ed. B. J. L. Cross (Melbourne, 1980), 73.

foundation for Newman himself, according to what is asserted in this passage, lies in his 'personal experience' of the obligation imposed by his conscience. There is no warrant for this assertion in anything he says. The experience he describes is the experience of a unique dictate bearing only upon what one is oneself to do, and do no matter what others may do to prevent it. Perhaps, though, it is not any experience of the 'obligation' or 'duty' to follow one's conscience, but this obligation or duty itself, which is pregnant with unsuspected consequences. 'Conscience has rights because it has duties' is something that Newman does say.

The two main questions taken up in this chapter are whether Newman attempts to derive rights of conscience from the duty or obligation of obedience to conscience, and whether rights of conscience are derivable from this duty or obligation. An enquiry as to whether Newman either commits himself to the view that conscience has rights of some kind in civil society or in the Church, or is committed unwittingly to a view on this matter, has to deal only with these questions; their discussion brings in all that is relevant. In particular, we do not have to look separately into possible implications of his ascription of authority to conscience, for this is explained by the magisterial character of the dictate of conscience and by the consequent duty of obedience to conscience. The authority of conscience is thus not something that might independently generate rights of conscience.

I

'Conscience has rights because it has duties.' Did Newman mean that rights of conscience, rights imposing a curb on the behaviour of others, are implied by duties of conscience? The words occur in the course of his argument to show what was and was not condemned in the condemnation of 'liberty of conscience' by two nineteenth-century popes. Their immediate setting is the following passage:

When men advocate the rights of conscience, they in no sense mean the right of the Creator, nor the duty to Him, in thought and deed, of the creature; but the right of thinking, speaking, writing, and acting, according to their judgment or their humour, without any thought of God at all. They do not even pretend to go by any moral rule . . . Conscience has rights because it has duties; but in this age, with a large portion of the public, it is the very right and freedom of conscience to dispense with conscience, to ignore a Lawgiver and Judge, to be independent of unseen obligations. It becomes a license to take up any or no religion . . . the right of self-will.[2]

Newman's words connecting rights of conscience with duties of conscience are taken by Eric D'Arcy, with no sign of hesitation, to state an argument: 'seeing that Conscience has duties, he firmly concludes that it has rights.'[3] D'Arcy goes on to emphasize the boldness of Newman in this matter. Up to the middle of the twentieth century very weighty theological opinion, he observes, allowed freedom of religion not as a right, but as 'a lesser evil'. 'Yet in 1875 Newman was already proclaiming both the right, and the limits of the right: and interpreting to that effect both Pope Gregory and Pope Pius.' The following passage from Newman is then quoted:

Both Popes certainly scoff at the 'so-called liberty of conscience,' but there is no scoffing of any Pope, in formal documents addressed to the faithful at large, at that most serious doctrine, the right and the duty of following that Divine Authority, the voice of conscience, on which in truth the Church herself is built.[4]

Our primary interest in any linking by Newman of rights and duties with conscience lies in whether he is attempting to derive rights of conscience from the duty of following conscience. There is no suggestion in this passage of inference from a duty to a right. There is, in fact, no suggestion in its use of the word 'right' of any kind of social right at all; 'right' and 'duty' form a linguistic unit with duty as its only clear meaning. Newman is not saying that the Church is founded on two things: a duty and a right (which the duty would imply). Nothing in what follows this passage needs to be noticed by us here; Newman goes on to themes discussed in a previous chapter, beginning with the pope's mission to sustain conscience and the dependence of the pope's rule on conscience.

[2] Letter to the Duke of Norfolk, § 5, p. 250.
[3] Eric D'Arcy, 'Conscience and Meta-Ethics', in *Shadows and Images*, p. 159.
[4] Letter to the Duke of Norfolk, § 5, p. 252.

'Rights of conscience' are maintained in the strongest terms in the following passage, but they are not social rights:

All through my day there has been a resolute warfare, I had almost said conspiracy, against the rights of conscience, as I have described it [as the primordial representative of God] . . . Chairs in Universities have been made the seats of an antagonist tradition. Public writers, day after day, have indoctrinated the minds of innumerable readers with theories subversive of its claims. As in Roman times and in the middle age, its supremacy was assailed by the arm of physical force, so now the intellect is put in operation to sap the foundations of a power which the sword could not destroy. We are told that conscience is but a twist in primitive and untutored man; that its dictate is an imagination; that the very notion of guiltiness, which that dictate enforces, is simply irrational . . . (Letter, § 5, p. 249)

The rights of conscience subject to the attack which Newman has described are not rights to do what conscience dictates, which others are to respect; it would be absurd to include among them a right to freedom or to dissent. An attack on the 'rights' or 'claims' of conscience which has it that conscience is 'but a twist in primitive and untutored man', or that the sense of guilt is irrational, is aimed at producing the belief that conscience is not what it claims to be.

Newman speaks of conscience as having 'the right of opposing the supreme, though not infallible Authority of the Pope' (Letter, § 5, p. 257). A few lines earlier he had spoken of the supreme authority of conscience in its own domain. The change to speaking of 'the right' of conscience to oppose the pope avoids the infelicity of a collision between two bearers of 'supreme authority', when the domain of conscience and that of the jurisdictional authority of the pope intersect (a mere infelicity since, as was noticed earlier, conscience and the pope do not have authority in the same sense of the word). The authority of conscience and the right it is here said to have equally terminate in one's own conduct.

In what we have been looking at, the rhetorical 'Conscience has rights because it has duties' alone suggests, and then in the vaguest way possible, any conception of rights of conscience with a social character. In what we are about to look at there is oblique evidence that Newman would have regarded the notion of rights of conscience which have prescriptive implications for the behaviour of others as having no connection with his way of thinking about conscience. He would not have been mistaken.

II

In the section of the Letter to the Duke of Norfolk following the one (§ 5) from which the material we have been considering is taken, a put-together right of conscience to all sorts of liberty is discussed. Newman's concern in this section is to explain and, in that way, justify condemnations issued by Pius IX in the encyclical *Quanta Cura* (1864), condemnations which in the standard denunciation of them by their critics, and by Gladstone in particular, appear as wholesale condemnations of the free exercise of religion, liberty of conscience, free speech, and a free press. Part of Newman's procedure removes incomprehensibility from Roman policy by disconcerting parallels with English constitutional arrangements, not altogether abrogated at the time at which he was writing.

> It was a first principle with England that there was one true religion, . . . that it came of direct Revelation, that it was to be supported to the disadvantage, to say the least, of other religions, of private judgment, of personal conscience . . . Men of the present generation, born in the new civilization, are shocked to witness in the abiding Papal system the words, ways, and works of their grandfathers. (Letter, § 6, pp. 262–3)

'When I was young the State had a conscience.'[5] But political reality (of which Newman had so acute a sense) has to be faced: if, instead of one conscience, the State has come to have 'half-a-dozen, or a score, or a hundred, in religious matters' (pp. 264, 267), a whole order of things has gone.

Directly defending the encyclical (the tone of which he

---

[5] Newman borrows a way of speaking recurrent in Gladstone's book *The State in its Relations with the Church* (1838). In this book the Anglican establishment in Ireland had been defended. ('It appears not too much to assume that our imperial legislature has been qualified to take . . . a sounder view of religious truth than the majority of the people in Ireland in their destitute and uninstructed state' (p. 80).)

greatly disliked), Newman points out that it does not proscribe, simply, liberty of conscience, of speech, of the press—any more than British law does. Newman turns to the proposition, the condemnation of which had for Gladstone, 'so frightful a meaning'. It is the following:

Liberty of conscience and worship, is the *inherent right* of all men. 2. It ought to be proclaimed in *every* rightly constituted society. 3. It is a right to *all sorts of liberty* (omnimodam libertatem) such, that it ought not to be restrained by any authority, ecclesiastical *or civil*, as far as public speaking, printing, or any other public manifestation of opinions is concerned.[6]

Is there 'any government on earth', Newman asks, that could stand the strain of such a doctrine as this? 'I say seriously Mr. Gladstone's accusation of us avails quite as much against Blackstone's four volumes, against laws in general, against the social contract, as against the Pope' (pp. 271, 273).

Throughout the discussion of the encyclical Newman's emphasis is upon the inescapability of limits on various liberties, not at all upon the value of the liberties themselves.[7] The explanatory defence of the encyclical made this emphasis appropriate. But after the exaltation of conscience in the previous section of the Letter, there might have been expected some expression of opinion that conscience, distinguished from its rights-demanding counterfeit, was to be treated with consideration. It is not to be found.

Early in the Letter, when measures against dissident religion in newly Christian imperial Rome are being commented upon, conscience happens to be mentioned, and what is said is this: 'I cannot get myself quite to believe that Pagans, Marcionites, and Manichees had much tenderness of conscience in their religious profession, or were wounded seriously by the Imperial rescript to their disadvantage' (§ 2, p. 203). 'The Novatians', it is added, 'certainly stand on higher ground.' But the inexorable conscience which members of this puritan sect must have had does nothing for it. Freedom of conscience, so

---

[6] Letter, § 6, p. 273 (Denzinger, No. 1690). The numbering and the emphases are Newman's. Part of the Latin is given in the Letter, p. 374 n.

[7] Elsewhere Newman can give liberty a very high place in the idea of the State: 'without power there is no protection, and without liberty there is nothing to protect' (*Discussions and Arguments*, pp. 317–18).

far from being given any grounding by Newman, is not so much as given a general endorsement.

III

Conceivably, however, Newman might have been logically committed to a view about rights of conscience which he did not actually hold and might have repudiated had it been put to him. Though he did not himself infer rights of conscience affecting the conduct of others from the duty of obedience to conscience, which he did maintain, such rights might be derivable from this duty. The argument which we are about to consider was developed by Eric D'Arcy in a book published in 1961 which has had a very considerable influence, *Conscience and its Right to Freedom*. It would presumably be this argument that D'Arcy saw as contained embryonically in Newman's saying that conscience has rights because it has duties.

The right of conscience to freedom which D'Arcy derives from the duty of obedience to conscience is a specific right. It is the right to what is often called simply 'freedom of conscience', the right to freedom from civil disabilities in the matter of religion. (Whether his argument would be arbitrarily restricted from implying a vastly more extensive right will be considered later on.) The right of conscience to freedom is a 'strict right'. A strict right is explained as being one which holds for the right-bearer's 'own benefit'. A right contractually acquired is an example of a strict right; the rights of a sovereign over his subjects are not rights in the strict sense, for they are held by the sovereign for the benefit of his subjects. Correlative with a strict right is a duty incumbent upon others to respect the right; the right holds 'against' them.

In order 'to establish the existence of a right', the argument begins, 'i.e. of a requirement of justice, in a given situation', 'we must show two things: first, that the subject in question has some ground for a claim on the object at issue; second, that he has not merely this ground, but the moral power to urge this as against some other person or persons'.[8] D'Arcy uses the example of a contract to illustrate the elements which he lists in the notion of a right. There is in a contract the 'object'—in a contract for professional services the object might be legal representation; there is the 'subject' in whom the right resides—in D'Arcy's example, the client (from whose point of view the contract is being looked at); there is the 'ground' of the right—in this example the client's agreement to pay for the lawyer's services; there is the 'party' to the contract against whom the right holds, the lawyer who has a 'strict duty' to render the services agreed upon (p. 204).

These elements D'Arcy finds present in the right of conscience to freedom. The subject of the right is everyone 'having the actual use of reason'. The object is 'an action, the following of one's conscience'. 'This involves immunity from external force compelling one to act against one's conscience', and 'immunity from external force denying one the ability to follow one's conscience' (p. 205). The ground on which the right of conscience to freedom is based is 'the absolute duty never to act against conscience' (p. 206). The party against whom the right is to hold is civil authority.

Two things have to be shown in order to establish the existence of a right. Not only must the ground for a claim to it be made out; there is also the matter of the 'moral power' to urge the claim. And the question now is whether the claim of conscience to freedom can be validly urged against the State. 'Could it be that there is some special feature of civil authority that renders it immune from or superior to the individual citizen's claim to freedom of conscience?' (p. 217). The argument then enters upon a discussion of the nature and purpose of the State, the upshot of which is that nothing renders the State immune from or superior to the claim of conscience.

A contract is used by D'Arcy only to illustrate the conceptual structure of a right (a right of the kind he ascribes to conscience, one to which there corresponds a duty on the part of others). He treats the right of conscience to freedom as

[8] Eric D'Arcy, *Conscience and its Right to Freedom* (London and New York, 1961), 204.

an 'essential human right'. (D'Arcy's argument is set within a
Thomist frame, and makes use of various Thomist considerations.) Essential human rights, unlike contractual rights,
'derive from the natural order itself, and belong to what St.
Thomas calls "natural justice"; the more intimately a given
"object" . . . is connected with the integrity of the human
personality, the more stringently is it protected by natural
justice' (p. 206). D'Arcy proceeds to characterize the status
assigned to one essential human right, the right to life, in
terms which are significant for an understanding of what is
going to be due to the right of conscience to freedom. Nothing
can 'abrogate' the right to life of the innocent; nothing can
justify its 'direct violation'. (Though 'absolute', this right is
not 'unlimited'; 'for the State may jeopardize life, i.e., permit
danger as a foreseen but unintended by-product . . . when
comparable goods are at stake', as happens when there is
military conscription in a war (p. 207). How high the right of
conscience to freedom comes in the scale of the more or less
stringently protected is made clear after some discussion that
need not be summarized. Its place is at the top of the scale,
above the right to life. The goal of each person's being is the
fulfilment of its various capacities, with a culminating
fulfilment in beatitude in a life to come. The integrity of one's
being and the attaining of this final perfection require

substantial fidelity to moral duty; and this . . . consists in following
one's conscience. Therefore the possibility of so following conscience
is a strict demand of natural justice. Where there is question of goods
that contribute helpfully, but not indispensably, to the integral
perfection of the human person, he has a conditional claim upon
them; it is conditional, namely, on its being compatible with the
comparable goods of other people; it can be subordinated to the
common good. But where there is question of goods that contribute
as necessary conditions to the sovereign end of the individual person,
the claim is unconditional; natural justice forbids its subordination
to any other end. St. Thomas instances our mortal life as being such
a good, and therefore as being so protected by natural justice; but
moral integrity is a greater good even than mortal life; therefore it
creates a still stronger claim to that which is needed for its
attainment, namely, the freedom to be faithful to the dictates of
conscience. (p. 214)

This passage in particular suggests that the argument we are considering is headed for a conclusion going far beyond the one it was designed to have. Why should the right of conscience to freedom, grounded upon the duty to follow conscience as a condition of obtaining one's highest good, be limited to freedom as regards religion, within civil society? Why should this consideration, if it can establish that freedom, not equally establish the right of conscience to freedom in every matter?

The argument contains a notion which can be used to insulate it against its having disastrous implications. This notion is that of the 'moral power' to urge a claim against individuals or institutions, without which a claim, however well-grounded, does not become a right. We can take it that the moral power to urge the claim is absent in the case of the enlargement of the right of conscience to freedom being contemplated.

There is, however, something dubious about an argument for the right of conscience to freedom, in the matter of religion, within civil society, if this specific freedom is the extent of the right which can be established on the basis of the entirely general consideration that fidelity to conscience is everyone's supreme need. Is there any principle on which a general right to freedom could be proposed for conscience? Certainly not if it is to be an 'absolute' right, never to be 'directly violated', or 'subordinated to the common good';[9] probably not, anyway: how would its permissions and restrictions differ from those of something long-familiar, a general right to liberty?

We turn to look at the 'duty' or 'obligation' from which the right of conscience to freedom is derived. It is a strange sort of duty. Holding whether or not the conscience is mistaken, it is a duty to do something whether right or wrong. As D'Arcy puts the difficulty: 'You seek to derive the right to do *x* from

---

[9] The characterization in these terms of the right of conscience to freedom as regards religious practice has every appearance of introducing impossibility into it also. Thugee and Suttee have to be stamped out by the State. Defending the proscription of practices such as these, D'Arcy keeps the right of conscience to religious freedom absolutely inviolable by taking in effect the line that they are not to count as demands on conscience (pp. 260–1).

the presence of a moral obligation to do x. But one cannot have a moral obligation to do what is wrong: for that would be tantamount to saying, x is both morally obligatory and morally wrong' (pp. 253–4). The difficulty is dealt with as follows:

To meet the objection one would point to the ambiguity latent in the term 'moral obligation'. Rights are derived, not immediately from what is *objectively* of moral obligation, but from what is subjectively so. For ultimately, rights are derived from and accounted for in terms of *ends and needs*; in so far as x is necessary for a person to attain his end, the sovereign end of personal existence, he has a right to x. Now, substantial fidelity to one's personal moral obligations is a necessary means to attaining one's end; this refers to what is *subjectively* one's obligation; and this in turn to that which one's conscience dictates . . . (p. 254)

It was remarked in the previous chapter—perhaps not guardedly enough—that the terms 'subjective obligation' and 'subjective duty', when used in connection with a mistaken conscience, were likely not to have the meaning they can strongly appear to have. They can look as though meant to designate an obligation or a duty, when all that is actually meant is likely to be that one takes oneself (whether mistakenly or not) to have an obligation or a duty. For the reply contained in this passage to the apposite to the objection it is to meet, however, the 'subjective obligation' spoken of has to be as real an obligation as an 'objective obligation', and not the mere taking of an obligation to exist. This reading of D'Arcy is supported by the occurrence of a sentence on the following page in which the viewing of something as a duty and the having of a subjective duty are not the same thing: 'Another man has no duty immediately with regard to the erroneous *view* itself, but to the *person* who mistakenly accepts it and does have a personal and subjective duty in its regard.'

The objection to deriving a right from the obligation to follow a mistaken conscience is that if this obligation exists, there would be an action which was 'both morally obligatory and morally wrong'. The reply is that the objection misses 'the ambiguity latent in the term "moral obligation" '. There is no contradiction in a person's being obliged—in one sense of the term—to do what, if his conscience is mistaken, he is obliged not to do—in another sense of the term.

The ambiguity in the term 'moral obligation' to which this reply takes itself to point is an invention of theory. For what are these two senses of the word 'obliged'? One sense is clear, at least it is if the word 'objectively' is removed from the word 'obliged'. We know what it is to be obliged to do something in virtue of an undertaking that has been given, or of some position of responsibility held; and because we do know this we are at a loss to understand what it is that we are being told, when it is that a person is obliged to do a thing in virtue of his taking himself to be obliged to do it. To speak of the duty of following conscience is to speak obfuscatingly. If you do have a certain duty and your conscience insists (against your reluctance) that you do it, you do not have two duties, one to do the thing, the other to obey your conscience. If, on the other hand, your conscience is mistaken, that is, if you do not have the duty you take yourself to have, you do not have in its place—magically—another one, 'a personal and subjective duty'. The reality behind the false suggestion conveyed when there is said to be a duty to follow a mistaken conscience would be expressed in exculpatory and (from a Last Judgement perspective) condemnatory judgements on persons. You are mistakenly convinced that something is your duty: it does not have to be in any sense your duty for you to act excusably in doing it or to deserve condemnation for not doing it.

An external consideration against supposing D'Arcy to have meant by 'a subjective obligation', or by 'a personal and subjective duty', an obligation or a duty and not merely the taking oneself to have this is implicit in a passage in his book *Human Acts*, published two years after *Conscience and its Right to Freedom*. He is criticizing part of the structure of Ross's theory of obligation (looked at in the previous chapter), the part where it is maintained that what we ought to do is determined not by the objective facts of the situation, but by what we take the facts to be. The criticism is, however, transferable to the notion that there is a duty to do what a mistaken conscience conceives to be a duty, a rightness in this situation in doing something that is wrong; and the indication given of what results when this notion and the language promoting it is cleared away is in line with what we have argued for. Rejecting the question 'Should one fulfil one's objective or subjective duty?' as containing 'a false suggestion', D'Arcy writes:

The person is not confronted with two versions of the facts between which he must choose; a person sees the facts only as *he* sees the facts, and not as someone else sees them. Nevertheless, someone else *can* see them; and an observer will often be in a position to say that the agent has acted on a false appraisal of the situation. Such an observer will not say of the mistaken man, 'He did his subjective duty'; but rather, 'He is excused for not doing his duty'. The description 'doing his subjective duty' incorporates a confusion of 'excuse' and 'justification'. The person who, after taking due care, arrives at a false appraisal of the facts is excused if he acts upon it; but his act is not *justified*; the act remains a wrongful act, but given the circumstances, the agent is not to be blamed for it.[10]

If, then, there is no duty (whether 'objective' or 'subjective'), in anything like the ordinary meaning of the word, to follow conscience, if assertions of this 'duty' to be plausible, or even intelligible, have to be radically recast, how would this affect the argument deriving a right from the duty to follow conscience? The ground of the right will become the need for substantial fidelity to what a person takes to be his duty, if he is to attain his supreme good. The need for the right will remain the same: fidelity to conscience is imperilled if a conscience has to face coercion or restraint. The problem constituted by the appearance of an action at once 'morally obligatory and morally wrong', if a mistaken conscience is to be followed, will not arise. All there would be is an action that was morally wrong but excusably done (and inexcusably not done), if dictated by a mistaken conscience. The right of conscience to freedom, however, will lose the appearance of having an adamantine foundation in duty. The freedom to which conscience will have a right will include freedom to do what is quite simply wrong.

[10] Eric D'Arcy, *Human Acts* (Oxford, 1963), 109–10.

IV

Newman's thought on the relation between religion and the State needs to be looked at more expansively than was possible when, earlier in the chapter, our attention was upon remarks he made in connection with the encyclical *Quanta Cura*. Our particular interest in obtaining a wider view of Newman's thought in this area is to see whether conscience becomes prominent at any point. An examination of aspects of a case built up to show that Newman came to favour 'the tolerant State, neutral on religious questions' will give us something of a perspective.

For Newman, Terence Kenny argues, the 'tolerant State, neutral on religious questions, was not something which had merely come about; it ought to have come about, and Newman found a justification for it in accordance with the political ideas he had long held'.[11] It is a question of some consequence whether it was a tolerant State, merely, that Newman might have come to favour or, more radically, a State neutral as regards religion. In either kind of State there is freedom of conscience in the matter of religion. If, then, starting out in his early Anglican days as a Tory, Newman came to favour a religiously neutral State rather than one that was merely tolerant of religious diversity, his preference for one over the other will not be due to a concern for freedom of conscience. (In the actuality of Kenny's argument 'tolerant' and 'religiously neutral' are best taken as synonymous and understood to mean the latter.) The dominating considerations Kenny sees at work in Newman's mind are not narrowly political. Their character is indicated by a variant statement at the end of the book of the proposition being argued for: 'the tolerant State not only might allowably come but must come and ought to come in a civilised society' (p. 191). The preferability, as Newman came to see it, of a religiously netural State to one with religious commitments is especially a matter of the preferability of civilization to barbarism. Thus one reads Kenny.

[11] Terence Kenny, *The Political Thought of John Henry Newman* (London, 1957), 18.

The contrast between barbarism and civilization drawn upon by Kenny is developed in the seventh lecture of a series on the history of the Turks, delivered by Newman in 1853. The feature of the contrast upon which Kenny fastens, for he obviously regards it as pregnant with significance for Newman's final view of the ideal relation between religion and the State, is the 'bond of union' within a society. Barbarian societies Newman sees as held together by 'objects of imagination', civilized societies by 'objects of sense'. 'Religion, superstition, belief in persons and families', he writes, 'objects, not proveable but vivid and imposing, will be the bond' which keeps together the members of a barbarian society.[12] Civilized societies 'ever tend to substitute objects of sense for objects of imagination as the basis of their existence' (Newman, p. 170; Kenny, p. 91). To communicate what he means by 'objects of sense' Newman turns to contemporary British society. 'At present, I suppose, our own political life as a nation lies in the supremacy of the law; and that again is resolvable into the internal peace, and protection of life and property, and freedom of the individual, which are its result; and these I call objects of sense' (Newman, p. 170; Kenny, p. 91). The 'ratiocinative habit', which Newman sees as both characteristic of civilized society and necessary to political progress, he sees as 'hostile to imagination and auxiliary to sense'.

A little earlier in the lecture Newman had brought a paean on civilization to this ending: 'Justice, benevolence, expedience, propriety, religion, are its recognized, its motive principles. Supernatural truth is its sovereign law. Such is it in its true idea, synonymous with Christianity; and not only in idea, but in matter of fact also, is Christianity ever civilization' (Newman, p. 165). The very considerable, if vague, difficulty this raises for the attribution to Newman of the view that the emergence of the religiously neutral State was desirable is in no way met by Kenny's remark—which was perhaps not intended to meet it—that the 'perfectly Christian State remains an ideal, never to be reached, limit' (Kenny, p. 92). In spite of the difficulty created by this identification of civilization 'in its true idea' with Christianity, the general impression resulting from the material Kenny presents is that

[12] History of the Turks, lect. 7, § 5; Historical Sketches, i. 171 (Kenny, p. 90).

Newman did not see religion in this lecture as the appropriate bond of union in a civilized State. An alternative bond (depending for its possibility on the character of a people, seen by Newman as unifying the British people) is 'the supremacy of the law'.[13]

Kenny's emphasis on the importance for Newman of the idea of law leads in one place to a misreading which ought to be mentioned because it could promote a very large misunderstanding of Newman's thought about conscience. He takes Newman to say there that in the course of human development conscience is necessarily replaced by law. Kenny even supplies Newman with a reason for this supersession:

The reason for the necessity of replacing conscience by law is not stressed, but it appears that it is not because conscience can thus be avoided, and wrong done with impunity, so much as that law gives a more certain and universal rule than a particular conscience; it can be viewed as a systemisation of the consciences of members of the State. (Kenny, p. 83)

The misunderstanding of Newman's thought this misreading could promote is the opposite of the usual one, which, ignoring his distinction between domains of authority, takes him simply to subordinate all external authority to conscience. Brought into conjunction with what is said in the Letter to the Duke of Norfolk of the fitfulness of conscience and of its liability to perversion, and so of its need for the light of revelation, this reading of Newman could suggest the view to someone disposed towards the radical reinterpretation of an author that if you look below the surface, you will find Newman totally subordinating conscience, not only to ecclesiastical, but also to civil authority.

The setting for the remarks which Kenny interprets as meaning that in the course of human development conscience is necessarily replaced by law is Newman's criticism (in connection with a characterization of Athenian society) of

[13] Compared with religion, 'the supremacy of the law' is an abstract social bond, as is indicated by the quotation in which the phrase occurs: the supremacy of the law is 'resolvable' into various things. And there is a great dependence of the law and the attitude to it on the 'national mind'. In 'Who's to Blame?' (1855) Newman speaks of the need for a 'continual influx of the national mind into the judicial conscience', of its being imperative that 'Public Opinion should give the law to Law' (Discussions and Arguments, p. 349).

three principles of conduct as 'substitutes' for conscience: 'Law, Expedience, and Propriety' (the Athenians, while not discarding law, and mindful of self-interest, choosing the third of these; professing 'to practise virtue on no inferior consideration, but simply because it was so praiseworthy, so noble and so fair'). Newman's remarks can now be left to speak for themselves. The rule of conscience is in

the divine order of things, but man,—not . . . over partial to so stern a reprover within his breast, yet seeing too the necessity of some rule or other, some common standard of conduct, if Society is to be kept together . . . as soon as he has secured for himself some little cultivation of intellect, looks about him how he can manage to dispense with Conscience, and find some other principle to do its work. The most plausible and obvious and ordinary of these expedients, is the Law of the State, human law; the more plausible and ordinary, because it really comes to us with a divine sanction, and necessarily has a place in every society or community of men.[14]

Features of Newman's criticism of what he referred to as the 'Christian Theocracy' of the Middle Ages have an important place in Kenny's argument to show that, in Newman's final view, the religiously neutral State is the best kind of State. The criticism is to be found in two letters written in 1860 to T. W. Allies, then engaged upon his book *The Formation of Christendom* (1865). The tendency of this criticism is to give a religious backing to the idea of a religiously neutral State. 'I do not see my way to hold', Newman wrote, 'that "Catholic Civilisation," as you describe it, is *in fact* (I do not say in the abstract), but in fact, has been, or shall be, or can be, a good, or *per se* desirable.'[15] Newman's reason (amplified in a second letter to Allies) is that through this fusion of the Church with society, the 'world' invades the Church. Is there anything grounded on claims of conscience in Newman's rejection of the medieval ideal? Nothing at all. Along with the Church and the 'world', the dominating theme is the 'salvation of souls'. Since 'the object of Christianity is to save souls; I ask, Have we reason to suppose that more souls were saved (relatively to the number of persons) under the Christian Theocracy

[14] Rise and Progess of Universities, ch. 7, in *Historical Sketches*, iii. 79.
[15] Newman to T. W. Allies, 22 Nov. 1860; *Letters and Diaries*, xix. 421 (Kenny, p. 134).

than under the Roman Emperors, or the English Georges?'
(p. 422).

In the second letter to Allies the salvation of souls is spoken
of in connection with one society after another, as though that
was all that mattered—the voice might almost be that of an
adherent of one of the evangelical sects. Newman speaks as
though he thought it no part at all of the mission of
Christianity to foster civilization. How, then, could he have
said that civilization 'in its true idea' is 'synonymous with
Christianity'? What appears in this letter as so wholly different
is, no doubt, to be seen as governed by the precise statement
of Newman's assumption at its beginning that 'the revealed
object of the institution of the Church, is to save souls'
(p. 430). The civilizing of society could hardly be thought of
as part of the content of revelation. Still, the fostering of
civilization by Christianity is not a theme of Newman's where
one might expect it to be, in *The Idea of a University* and in
the Rise and Progress of Universities.

Making the absence of this theme more noticeable is the
providential character assigned to civilization in the lecture
'Christianity and Letters' (1854). The 'association of intellect
and mind' which had developed in the countries surrounding
the Mediterranean, Newman thought, had a special claim to
be called Civilization, and the part of the world it unified to be
called the World. In God's ordering of things the coming of
the Christian religion was delayed until Civilization had
reached its perfect form. Civilization is directed to the service
of the Christian religion; co-operation between them is
mentioned, but the impression given is of the self-contained
excellence of Civilization.[16] A theme in the ninth discourse of
The Idea of a University indicates the perception of an
impossibility in the notion of a Christian civilization. 'Literature
is to man in some sort what autobiography is to the individual;
it is his Life . . . the Life . . . of the *natural* man, innocent or
guilty.' 'On the whole, then, I think it will be found, and ever
found, as a matter of course, that Literature, as such, no
matter of what nation, is the science or history, partly and
at best of the natural man, partly of man in rebellion'
(pp. 227–8).

[16] *The Idea of a University* (2nd edn., 1859), 227–8, 251–4.

Newman did, however, see a civilizing influence as part of the effect of Christianity, if not of its mission. And liberty, he believes, was something it had in effect fostered. 'You attribute freedom of thought and action, not to Christianity, not to "the faith and virtues of the Christians" but to the stream of barbaric migration,' Newman wrote to Lord Acton, commenting upon a point in Acton's lecture 'The History of Freedom in Christianity' (1877). 'Of course I would not deny', he continues that 'when Christianity was some centuries old, the Teutonic element co-operated in "the history of freedom"; but did not Christianity itself commence the emancipation of the individual mind by informing the law of conscience and of faith? Were not the Martydoms in the first centuries a portentous novelty, bringing in a new world? and did not Hosius, Hilary . . . follow up that heroic revolution by their free words and acts in a matter of opinion', in defiance of emperors? (In the first of Acton's Lectures on Modern History (1899–1901), in more pronounced contrast with Newman, conscience leading to liberty is seen as nurtured not by, but from within institutional Christianity. Conscience came to be spoken of in the thirteenth century as 'the audible voice of God, that never misleads or fails, that ought to be obeyed always whether enlightened or darkened, right or wrong'. The 'secret monitor' was depressed at first below 'public and visible authority'; but as coercion declined, 'the claim of Conscience rose, and the ground abandoned by the inquisitor was gained by the individual'.)[17]

Though he valued things in the medieval civilization of Europe—among them its freedom in theological investigation[18]—Newman was certainly no celebrant of the civilization Christianity most inspired.[19] His attitude towards

[17] Newman to Acton, 16 June 1877; *Letters and Diaries*, xxviii. 206; Acton, 'The History of Freedom in Christianity', repr. in *The History of Freedom and Other Essays*, ed. J. N. Figgis and R. V. Laurence (London, 1907), 31; *Lectures on Modern History*, ed. Figgis and Laurence (London, 1906), 31–2.

[18] 'Why was it that the Medieval Schools were so vigorous? Because . . . the disputants were not made to feel the bit in their mouths at every other word they spoke . . . if the dispute got perilous . . . then at length Rome intervened—at length, not at first—Truth is wrought out by many minds working together freely' (Newman to Robert Ornsby, 26 Mar. 1863; *Letters and Diaries*, xx. 426).

[19] An impression, partly misleading and partly illuminating, of Newman's view of the relation of an aspect of medieval civilization to his own time and work is given in

another civilization—British civilization in the nineteenth century—is important for an attempt to determine what he came to think of as the best kind of State. It is easy to believe on reading 'Who's to Blame?' (a series of letters Newman wrote for a Catholic newspaper, occasioned by British performance in the Crimean War) that he would have preferred living in mid-nineteenth-century England to living in any other State, then or in the past. But since preferability and not personal preference is the issue, the significance of an irony in his discussion of its arrangements for religion should not be missed. Just as the peacetime army of England has certain deprivations inflicted upon it, so does its 'religious establishment'. 'The Constitutional Spirit allows to the troops arms and ammunition, as it allows to the clergy Ordination and two sacraments, neither being really dangerous' in the absence of accessories required for their efficiency.[20] So far as any inference is to be drawn, it looks as if it would be in line with the inference to be drawn from Newman's criticism of medieval civilization. This is that the establishment of religion is harmful to religion. And in a letter written some years later, in connection with religious persecution in Spain, he says: 'I

Culler's great study of his educational philosophy, *The Imperial Intellect*. The work of the Middle Ages, which Culler says Newman 'regarded his own work as repeating in some sense', was the harmonizing of new thought with traditional thought and belief; he saw the 19th cent. as faced with the same problem as the 12th (A. Dwight Culler, *The Imperial Intellect* (New Haven, 1955), 251–2). The Rise and Progress of Universities is cited. Written (at an elementary level) in connection with the founding of a Catholic university in Ireland, this composition indicates no other consciousness of medieval civilization, which produced the first universities, than its occasion would suggest. The significance of the little it contains relevant to the harmonizing theme can be gauged from the following remark: 'Happy age, whatever its other inconveniences, happy so far as this, that religion and science were then a bond of union' (p. 176). Aquinas is barely mentioned. Culler was symbolizing Newman's work by the work of the Middle Ages, not communicating Newman's own sense of it. A form of the harmonizing theme is very prominent in *The Idea of a University*. Its prominence, and Newman's speaking in connection with it of an 'Architectonic Science or Philosophy' (*Idea*, 4th Discourse, pp. 90–1), lead Culler to look for medieval antecedents and to say that 'philosophy was regarded by Newman as the study appropriate to . . . the nineteenth century' (*Imperial Intellect*, p. 251). Diffident about his knowledge of philosophy, and not much liking what he knew of contemporary philosophy, Newman could not have regarded philosophy, as a subject, in that light. I. T. Ker argues convincingly in the introduction to his edition of *The Idea of a University* (Oxford, 1976), pp. lv–lvii, that the architectonic science is no more than a certain 'habit of mind'.

[20] 'Who's to Blame?', in *Discussions and Arguments*, pp. 358–9.

am not at all sure that it would not be better for the Catholic religion every where, if it had no very different status from that which it has in England. There is so much corruption, so much deadness . . . when a dogmatic faith is imposed on a nation by law, that I like freedom better.'[21]

The nature of the religious consideration at least primarily inclining Newman to favour the emergence of the religiously neutral State is clear. It is not that diversity of religion should be tolerated; it is that religion is invaded by its establishment. In what we have been looking at no concern for the interests of conscience has shown up.

A tendency in Newman to favour the emergence of the religiously neutral State is all that can be proved. The intrinsic preferability of this kind of State to any other, in Newman's judgement, certainly could not be inferred from the Letter to the Duke of Norfolk; its desirability, given 'the feelings of the age', might be.

Two remarks, both made a few years before the Letter to the Duke of Norfolk, both of about the same date, show Newman pulled in opposite directions as to the ideal relation between religion and the State. 'I should call myself an Anti-Liberal', he says in the first of these remarks,

because, in harmony with the Pope's syllabus, I should say that the best thing of all is to have a Unity of religion in a country and that so *real* that its Ascendancy is but the expression of the universal mind.[22]

'Though it be true abstractedly', he says in the second remark,

that the true religion alone is to be allowed, yet in the concrete it is allowable to wish that there should be a general toleration of all religions.[23]

The wish expressed in this second remark might have been more real to Newman than the balancing abstraction. In deeper accordance with his mind, however, than the opinion expressed in either of these remarks is the view that there is no abstract best in the relation between religion and the State, that what is best is only what is best in the circumstances.

---

[21] Newman to William Monsell, 17 June 1863; *Letters and Diaries*, xx. 477.

[22] Newman to Richard Frederick Clarke, 20 Dec. 1868; ibid. xxiv. 340.

[23] *Theological Papers of John Henry Newman on Biblical Inspiration and Infallibility*, ed. J. Derek Holmes (Oxford, 1979), 101. The editorial introduction suggests 1865 as the probable date for the paper from which this quotation comes.

V

At the beginning of this chapter Newman is represented in a remarkable quotation as taking for granted that if conscience is so great that it must always be followed, it must possess rights commensurate with its greatness. What in fact is to be found in his writing is not something more moderate: it is his apparently taking for granted that no rights at all accrue to conscience in virtue of its always having to be followed, his proceeding as though it would never cross anyone's mind that they did. There is a clear ascription of rights to conscience in the Letter to the Duke of Norfolk, but they are not rights of the kind in question, rights holding against others, whether individuals or institutions, binding them to let conscience be freely followed. They are rights holding, so to speak, against oneself: the attack on them described by Newman at some length is not aimed at curtailing freedom of conscience, but at reducing the demands of conscience upon oneself to groundless feeling. The rights which conscience has 'because it has duties' would be rights of the kind in question—social rights—but their mention serves only a rhetorical purpose. If Newman believed that any rights of conscience exist, with correlative duties towards it on the part of others, there was an occasion in the Letter seriously calling for some expression of this belief: called for when he defended the papal condemnation of a proposition claiming the right of conscience to 'all sorts of liberty' was an affirmation, however oblique, of some right of conscience to liberty. There is none. In a more general survey of Newman's thought about religion in relation to the State we came upon no affirmation of the need for political arrangements suitable to the interests of conscience.

How is to be explained, then, that Newman can seem to some of his readers to be a very strong proponent of rights of conscience? The explanation is that they bring to their reading of him the assumption that if conscience must be followed, it must have rights.

Newman did not see conscience as having rights of the kind supposed. The question arises, however, as to whether he might have been blind to a connection that actually exists: their entailment by the duty of obedience to conscience. We discussed an argument designed to show that the 'absolute duty' of obedience to conscience carries with it a right of conscience to freedom from civil disabilities in the matter of religion. Holding whether or not a conscience is mistaken, this 'duty' would in some cases be a duty to do something whether right or wrong. One way in which an action can be wrong is by its being an invasion of the rights of others. There is nothing to stop a conscience dictating an action of that kind, nor anything to stop an action of that kind from being required in some religion. Yet the right of conscience to freedom, which was to follow from the duty of obedience to conscience and was on no argued grounds contracted to religious freedom, was to be an 'absolute' right, one never to be 'directly violated'.

To have inviolable, sacrosanct rights would accord with the awful, uncompromising character of conscience; but consciences collide, and people have to live together. The inference to be drawn is not that conscience has more moderate rights, but that the category of rights is inappropriately invoked in connection with its dictates. What can be asked for on behalf of conscience from those affected by its action is as much consideration as circumstances permit. And it might seem surprising that Newman's assertion of the need for obedience to conscience at all costs is unaccompanied by any indication that he thought conscience had a claim on the goodwill of others, arising out of this need. The fact is that the claims of conscience monopolizing his attention were its claims upon oneself.

CONCLUDING REMARKS

I

NEWMAN assigned to conscience the direction and rule of one's own conduct. According to his most detailed account of its nature, conscience is at once 'a moral sense' and the source of 'a magisterial dictate'; determining an action to be right or wrong, it commands or prohibits the doing of it accordingly. In Newman's view the deliverances of conscience in the direction of conduct are always particular, prescribing what is to be done as right or avoided as wrong in the actual circumstances in which one finds oneself. This particularity is a premiss in his obscure argument to show that conscience cannot be involved in collision with teaching put forward by the Church as infallible: the teaching, and the deliverances of conscience in their particularity, have different domains. So its justification is an important question, one to be resolved only by reference to the ordinary conception of conscience. But, whatever the significance of the most obscure element in his argument—the apparent contrast between a direct and an indirect collision—the mere particularity of the deliverances of conscience will not prevent an intersection of domains. If it belongs to conscience to determine right and wrong at all, though only in fully detailed circumstances and only for oneself, the possibility of collision opens up. So again, what comes within the scope of conscience, in the ordinary conception of it, is a matter with a decisive bearing on his argument.

While Newman saw conscience in its superintendency of conduct as having a double operation, determinative of right and wrong and imperatival, his emphasis is on conscience as imperatival. As such, conscience is 'one and the same in the mind of every one'. It is as imperatival that its dictates present themselves magisterially, as if an 'echo' or 'reverberation' of the voice of God in command and prohibition, and as giving felt testimony to their having behind them a divine 'sanction'. In Newman's phenomenology of conscience, as distinct from his abstract account of it, conscience does not so much as have a determinative aspect (because, of course, nothing is characteristically experienced when something is judged to be right or wrong). So he does not direct us towards finding within ourselves any testimony from conscience with respect to the determinations of right and wrong he saw it as making, which would correspond to what invests its imperatival dictates with authority. Only with some doubtfulness, in fact, is he to be read as really intending to ascribe authority to conscience in this connection.

It is argued in this essay that to ascribe authority to conscience in the determination of right and wrong is altogether misconceived. If that conclusion is soundly reached, the failure of Newman's attempt to demonstrate the impossibility of collision between conscience and teaching put forward by the Church as infallible will not have left two *authorities* in confrontation. Assuming that it is from conscience that a judgement inconsistent with something in this teaching proceeds, there is only one authority on the scene: that of the Church. Assuming that such a judgement lies beyond the scope of conscience, this is still true; for if the judgement cannot properly be regarded as delivered by that conceptually circumscribed aspect of oneself which is conscience, it is made by oneself. And no ordinary person is an authority in matters of right and wrong.

It is not any authority which Newman might have seen conscience as having in the determination of right and wrong he assigns to it that is brought into relation with the authority of the Church. The authority of conscience—its 'supreme authority' over each person's own conduct—brought by Newman into this relationship, specifically with the authority of the pope, is its authority of command and prohibition. Within 'the domain of action', the collision, which Newman saw as impossible over teaching, can take place, the dictate of conscience colliding with some dictate of papal jurisdiction. But the appearance is produced of collision between supreme authority and supreme authority.

This appearance is dissolved by the assumption that conscience and the pope do not have authority in the same sense. The context suggests a meaning for the authority for which a meaning has to be found, which, of course, is that of conscience. No question arises as to what is to be understood by the authority of the pope. When Newman spoke of this authority, he was speaking of what was established by the constitution of the Church and by ecclesiastical arrangements. As juxtaposed to the authority of the pope, the authority of conscience will be the 'duty' of obedience to conscience. (How such a 'duty' is itself to be understood is one of the main concerns in the essay.) We have to go beyond the context in which Newman asserts the duty to find his grounding for it, and make a connection which he does not himself explicitly make. We have to go back to his description of the quality of the dictate of conscience as uniquely magisterial, constraining us 'like no other dictate in the whole of our experience'. In the experienced quality of this dictate, along with the phenomena of an accusatory or condemnatory conscience, the title of conscience to obedience, to rule our conduct, is manifested; and the ascription of authority to conscience at once invested with meaning and justified.

The authority of conscience in this account of it is over what one *does*. Now, if, as Newman held, it belongs to the office of conscience, not only to command and prohibit actions, but also to determine what to command and prohibit, it can, contrary to what he held, find itself in collision with the Church's teaching, even with teaching put forward as infallible. But no schism opens up in his thought with the failure of his argument to show the impossibility of this collision. With its occurrence there are three possibilities: to set oneself to believe with the Church, to do nothing, to leave the Church. (Whatever might have been Newman's opinion of the second and third of these possibilities is of incidental significance; all three are compatible with his conception of conscience and with the ordinary conception of it.) Conscience maintains its authority over one's conduct whichever of these possibilities is settled for because thought right. The authority of conscience does not presuppose consistency, nor any more integrity than consciousness can ascertain. The authority of the Church is, of course, unaffected whatever one does. Conscience and the Church do not have authority in the same sense.

Newman has been interpreted as inferring rights of conscience from the 'duty' of obedience to conscience in all circumstances. His remarks, it is argued, will not bear this interpretation. And with this interpretation set aside, he reappears as seeing this duty only as one to be carried out at whatever cost to oneself. That it had no implications as to what ought to exist within civil society or the Church he seems to have taken entirely for granted. It is argued that it could have no implications of the kind to which he might have been inadvertently committed. In the impression somehow existing that Newman's thought about conscience makes him especially significant for our time, rights of conscience is a prominent notion. In fact, his thought about conscience does not make him significant for our time more than for any other. Specifically, he did not see himself as putting forward any new ideas on the claims of conscience within the Church; nor was he.

Beginning with Chapter 4 of the essay, the discussion off and on, incidentally and by implication, has a bearing on how Newman's remark should be taken, that in an after-dinner toast he would drink to conscience first and then to the pope. It should be taken as just a remark. The inferences it might suggest are not to be drawn from it. No inferences are to be drawn from it.

II

For the most part Newman's thought about conscience is not his best thought. To a large extent this is due to the subject, and to his commitments with regard to it. The fixed assumption that conscience is a 'simple element' in our make-up, not 'resolvable into more elementary principles', greatly diminishes the possibilities open to an account of the nature of conscience. Fully aware of the extent to which this assumption was under contemporary attack, Newman attempted no defence of it. The point is not that he left a piece of work incomplete: being exemplified are the limitations imposed on his thought when brought to bear on conscience. It is doubtful whether a general defence of the assumption that conscience is an original element in the constitution of the mind is possible; all that might be open to anyone making the assumption is criticism of specific developmentalist theories of conscience.

That our ability to reach moral truth depends greatly upon our moral disposition, and that our ability to reach religious truth depends greatly upon our moral and religious dispositions, were 'first principles' with Newman. Newman's first principles are not propositions which present themselves as abstractly obvious. They are reached by abstraction from particular experiences. Of more importance, they are not always grasped in their particular exemplification by a bare seeing or sensing; they are sometimes distillations of a way of life, as these two principles are. There is an early limit on the possibilities of making out an intellectual case for principles of this character. The principle that there is a dependence of moral perception on moral disposition would meet with wide agreement (though beneath the agreement there would be disagreement about the nature of moral truth). Only anti-religious prejudice would dismiss the other principle out of hand as an expression of religious prejudice. But its very claim makes it a principle— to recall the old term—of 'experimental religion'. And for Newman, that religious truth is not to be apprehended in the absence of the appropriate moral and religious dispositions is much more than a principle recording an epistemological fact; it is a fundamental principle of religion. (The title of one of his sermons is 'Truth hidden when not sought after'.) No criticism, then, is being made of him for failure to set out a convincing case for the principle, addressed alike to believer and unbeliever. Attention is being drawn again to the theoretical intractability of material he had to work with in his philosophy of conscience.

Both principles make an appearance in the description contained in the *Grammar of Assent* of what, as is shown by Newman's account of it, lies at the limit of possible description: how we actually do reason in 'concrete matters'. This reasoning proceeds by the accumulation of considerations arising out of the circumstances of the particular case, considerations 'too fine to avail separately', and incapable of 'verbal enumeration', considerations many of which will weigh differently with different persons; it does not proceed step by step, but is influenced by all of these considerations together in an unanalysable summing up. Newman's description of this reasoning is the most sustained example of a characteristic method in the communication of his thought, the setting out of something in a way designed to evoke the response 'Yes, that is how it is.' What is set out in this description is called by Newman 'matter of fact', and what comes into view in the course of it is not a dependence of our ability to reach moral and religious truth on our moral and religious dispositions, as hardly needs saying, but the matter of fact that as these dispositions are present or absent, so accordingly will various considerations be weighed differently.

'All Newman's writing was intensely personal, a conversation with sympathisers.'[1] This remark can be used to indicate a standpoint from which to make one kind of appraisal of Newman's writing. Newman, of course, wrote to convince. And an appraisal of his writing can be made by asking how far it has to depend upon a reader's sympathy to be effective in this way, meaning by 'sympathy', not any appeal of Newman's personality or cast of mind; specifying as its meaning shared belief. With this question in view, let us look back at one of the most important things in Newman's philosophy of conscience, the transition he conducts from the phenomena of conscience to belief in God as a reality.

A question arises with regard to the phenomena themselves: specifically with regard to the sense of a uniquely constraining imperative, and the sense of foreboding following upon transgression. The question is whether this sense of a unique constraint and the presence of foreboding among the phenomena of a bad conscience do not both presuppose theistic belief rather than, as Newman held, enabling it to be engendered. (Slightly adapting a query in his *Philsophical Notebook*, the question might be obliquely asked, by asking whether 'the Chinese' have these experiences.) Do the phenomena in

---

[1] P. A. Kasteel in his introduction to Zeno's *John Henry Newman: Our Way to Certitude* (Leiden, 1957), p. v.

question presuppose for their existence some degree of theistic belief? It would be most surprising if this was so. There must be many people who have lost belief in God, and experience the phenomena. But past belief may be necessary, though present belief is not. (The past belief is perhaps not necessarily that of the individual; conceivably the phenomena could exist as a sort of cultural deposit, preserved by ways of speaking about conscience that linger on.)

Grant Newman's description of the phenomena of conscience. Let it be allowed, that is, that the description would be concurred in by a reader as corresponding to what he finds within himself, even if part of this he would not have altogether found by himself, had it been left undescribed. What now happens is at once an evocation and an argument. The insistent *intimations* of the phenomena are evoked, and a similar concurrence of the reader expected; at the same time, on the basis of a correlativity of certain states of mind with what Newman refers to as 'personal objects', *implications* of the phenomena are specified. The argument is weak; the evocation powerful—on a supposition. This supposition is that the reader share with Newman to some degree a belief in God. Then, as a result of his reflecting on the phenomena to which his attention has been drawn and which have been made articulate, his belief might indeed change in character, lose mere notionality, and take on reality. Perhaps the supposition is stated too strongly: apprehension that there might be a God might be sufficient. And perhaps sometimes a different shared belief would enable more to be effected than this conversion of the character of an already existing belief. Not already having any belief in God, but believing with Newman that conscience is 'an original principle' in our nature—that no story of interiorized human commands and prohibitions will explain the unique quality of its dictates or its forebodings—he might find himself concurring in Newman's account of what is intimated by the phenomena of conscience and might be led to a belief in God.

The limited possibilities of his material, coupled with the restrictions imposed by certain commitments of his own with respect to it, do not fully explain why Newman, writing on conscience, is not, on the whole, at his best. Improbable as naïvety in him might seem to be, it is conspicuously present in his handling of the notion of a moral sense. And the power to reason which he attributes to conscience is left wholly unrelated to its power of moral-sense perception. But where expectations based on familiarity with his other work are most notably defeated is in the argument in the Letter to the Duke of Norfolk that would show the impossibility of collision between conscience and teaching put forward by the Church as infallible. This is not because the argument fails; it is mainly because it is so difficult to make out what the argument is. Obscurities, unrelatedness, incompleteness in Newman's writing on conscience are very largely due to its incidental character: it is ancillary to his treatment of other matters; he had no occasion to bring together various parts of his thought about conscience. His most extended treatment of the nature of conscience (which covers a few pages) is subordinated to showing how a living belief in God is possible. The argument, insulating conscience from an encounter with infallible teaching, is a quickly taken step in another argument. There is no need to go outside the Letter to the Duke of Norfolk for a powerful contrast with the quality of its section on conscience. It is provided by Newman's discussion of the political significance of the Vatican decrees. With this particularly in mind, H. J. Laski wrote of the Letter: 'It remains with some remarks of Sir Henry Maine and a few brilliant dicta of F. W. Maitland as perhaps the profoundest discussion of obedience and of sovereignty in the English language.'[2] No sympathy of belief as between writer and reader is necessary to render convincing what Newman maintains regarding the political significance of the decrees. And the same thing is substantially true of the argument in the *Apologia* and in the *Essay on the Development of Doctrine*, which has often changed a person's beliefs.

The great Newman as a writer is the traditionally great Newman, the Newman of the *Apologia*, of the *Essay*, and of the Letter in its treatment of the theme of Church and State: and the Newman of the Sermons—of the *Parochial and Plain Sermons*, rather than of the *University Sermons*. His thought about conscience is, of course, important, though most of it

[2] H. J. Laski, *Studies in the Problem of Sovereignty* (New Haven, 1917; repr. 1968), 202.

more because it is his than because of what he is able to do with a subject-matter of limited theoretical interest. Making it particularly important as Newman's thought is the question of its unity with his thought about the Church. Neither directly nor by implication, it is argued in this essay, are these two areas of Newman's thought in conflict.

INDEX